GROVER E. MURRAY
STUDIES IN THE
AMERICAN SOUTHWEST

Also in the series:

Agaves, Yuccas, and Their Kin: Seven Genera of the Southwest, by Jon L. Hawker

Between Two Rivers: Photographs and Poems Between the Brazos and the Rio Grande, by Jerod Foster and John Poch

Brujerías: Stories of Witchcraft and the Supernatural in the American Southwest and Beyond, by Nasario García

Cacti of Texas: A Field Guide, by A. Michael Powell, James F. Weedin, and Shirley A. Powell

Cacti of the Trans-Pecos and Adjacent Areas, by A. Michael Powell and James F. Weedin

Cowboy Park: Steer-Roping Contests on the Border, by John O. Baxter

Dance All Night: Those Other Southwestern Swing Bands, Past and Present, by Jean A. Boyd

Dancin' in Anson: A History of the Texas Cowboys' Christmas Ball, by Paul H. Carlson

Deep Time and the Texas High Plains: History and Geology, by Paul H. Carlson

"Don't Count the Tortillas": The Art of Texas Mexican Cooking, by Adán Medrano

Equal Opportunity Hero: T.J. Patterson's Service to West Texas, by Phil Price

Finding the Great Western Trail, by Sylvia Gann Mahoney

From Texas to San Diego in 1851: The Overland Journal of Dr. S. W. Woodhouse, Surgeon-Naturalist of the Sitgreaves Expedition, edited by Andrew Wallace and Richard H. Hevly

The Frontier Centennial: Fort Worth and the New West, by Jacob W. Olmstead

Grasses of South Texas: A Guide to Identification and Value, by James H. Everitt, D. Lynn Drawe, Christopher R. Little, and Robert I. Lonard

A Haven in the Sun: Five Stories of Bird Life and Its Future on the Texas Coast, by B. C. Robison

A Kineño's Journey: On Learning, Family, and Public Service, by Lauro F. Cavazos, with Gene B. Preuss

Kit Carson and the First Battle of Adobe Walls: A Tale of Two Journeys, by Alvin R. Lynn

In the Shadow of the Carmens: Afield with a Naturalist in the Northern Mexican Mountains, by Bonnie Reynolds McKinney

Javelinas: Collared Peccaries of the Southwest, by Jane Manaster

Land of Enchantment Wildflowers: A Guide to the Plants of New Mexico, by LaShara J. Nieland and Willa F. Finley

Little Big Bend: Common, Uncommon, and Rare Plants of Big Bend National Park, by Roy Morey

Lone Star Wildflowers: A Guide to Texas Flowering Plants, by LaShara J. Nieland and Willa F. Finley

More Than Running Cattle: The Mallet Ranch of the South Plains, by M. Scott Sosebee

My Wild Life: A Memoir of Adventures within America's National Parks, by Roland H. Wauer

Myth, Memory, and Massacre: The Pease River Capture of Cynthia Ann Parker, by Paul H. Carlson and Tom Crum

Opus in Brick and Stone: The Architectural and Planning Heritage of Texas Tech University, by Brian H. Griggs

Pecans: The Story in a Nutshell, by Jane Manaster

Picturing a Different West: Vision, Illustration, and the Tradition of Austin and Cather, by Janis P. Stout

Plants of Central Texas Wetlands, by Scott B. Fleenor and Stephen Welton Taber

Seat of Empire: The Embattled Birth of Austin, Texas, by Jeffrey Stuart Kerr

Texas Natural History in the 21st Century, by David J. Schmidly, Robert D. Bradley, and Lisa C. Bradley

Texas, New Mexico, and the Compromise of 1850: Boundary Dispute and Sectional Crisis, by Mark J. Stegmaier

Texas Quilts and Quilters: A Lone Star Legacy, by Marcia Kaylakie with Janice Whittington

Truly Texas Mexican: A Native Culinary Heritage in Recipes, by Adán Medrano

The Wineslinger Chronicles: Texas on the Vine, by Russell D. Kane

BLACKDOM, NEW MEXICO

THE SIGNIFICANCE OF THE AFRO-FRONTIER, 1900–1930

TIMOTHY E. NELSON
FOREWORD BY HERBERT G. RUFFIN II

TEXAS TECH UNIVERSITY PRESS

Copyright © 2023 by Timothy E. Nelson

All rights reserved. No portion of this book may be reproduced in any form or by any means, including electronic storage and retrieval systems, except by explicit prior written permission of the publisher. Brief passages excerpted for review and critical purposes are excepted.

This book is typeset in EB Garamond. The paper used in this book meets the minimum requirements of ANSI/NISO Z39.48-1992 (R1997). ♾

Designed by Hannah Gaskamp

Library of Congress Cataloging-in-Publication Data

Names: Nelson, Timothy E., author. Title: Blackdom: The Significance of the Afro-Frontier, 1900–1930 / Timothy E. Nelson. Other titles: Grover E. Murray Studies in the American Southwest. Description: Lubbock, Texas: Texas Tech University Press, [2023] | Series: Grover E. Murray Studies in the American Southwest | Includes bibliographical references and index. | Summary: "A multifaceted look at the freedman township of Blackdom, New Mexico that repositions the community on the history of the American frontier."—Provided by publisher.
Identifiers: LCCN 2022061692 (print) | LCCN 2022061693 (ebook) |
ISBN 978-1-68283-175-5 (paperback) | ISBN 978-1-68283-176-2 (ebook)
Subjects: LCSH: Frontier and pioneer life—New Mexico—Blackdom—African Americans. | African Americans—New Mexico—History. | Blackdom (N.M.)—History.
Classification: LCC F802.C5 N45 2023 (print) | LCC F802.C5 (ebook) |
DDC 978.9/43—dc23/eng/20230213
LC record available at https://lccn.loc.gov/2022061692
LC ebook record available at https://lccn.loc.gov/2022061693

Printed in the United States of America
23 24 25 26 27 28 29 30 31 / 9 8 7 6 5 4 3 2 1

Texas Tech University Press
Box 41037
Lubbock, Texas 79409-1037 USA
800.832.4042
ttup@ttu.edu
www.ttupress.org

This is for the Pastors, Patriarchs and *Positioned*. There are those who endure in silence to maintain community. Instead of a silent death, they live a loud prayer life. Above all, they keep showing up, day in and day out. Three years of a global pandemic and upheaval; leadership matters. Thank you for leadership in times of tumult.

Posthumously, I would like to thank Dr. Maceo Crenshaw Dailey. Although Dr. Dailey passed away prior to my dissertation defense and graduation, he endured me. He prepared me enough and left me with a mentor: Dr. Selfa A. Chew-Melendez. Hopefully, Dr. John D. Marquez can recognize his influence on my work. Last but not least, Dr. Antonio Lopez, thank you for your peer mentorship.

CONTENTS

FOREWORD

In the US West, the history of African Americans is not just a footnote. Their story is a major part of the events, meaning, and significance of American life. This is especially true when one considers the arcs of both urban and civil rights history that have dominated the field since the early 1990s in publications such as Albert Broussard's *Black San Francisco* (1993). But that record is not in the canon of Black New Mexico history. In 2000, the overall state of the field was addressed at the two-day Smithsonian Institution symposium "A Quest for Freedom: The Black Experience in the American West" (Washington, DC, 2001). This conference was organized by the Program of African American Culture at the National Museum of American History. Its committee included keynote speaker Quintard Taylor, chair Lonnie Bunch, and coordinators Alonzo Smith and myself. The most critical areas of this symposium against which to test the field's significance are those that centrally intersect Timothy E. Nelson's *Blackdom, New Mexico: The Significance of the Afro-Frontier, 1900–1930* in "America's Racial Frontier" and "Exploding Myths of the Frontier." After hearing from the most prolific scholars in the field, at the conference's end most panelists agreed that African American western scholarship had finally evolved beyond being what Taylor had conceptualized—in his groundbreaking book *In Search of the Racial Frontier* (1998)—as moving from being merely a "footnote" towards a period of significance.

In the broader scope of the African American West, *Blackdom* is informed by black western scholars Kenneth M. Hamilton and Quintard Taylor. Central to Hamilton's work on *Black Towns and Profit* (1991) was finding significance in Black Town formation through Black entrepreneurship in Nicodemus (Kansas), Mound Bayou (Mississippi), Langston City and Boley (Oklahoma), and Allensworth (California). Whereas, essential to Taylor's work are Black community formation; the significance of African American westerners' history and culture; the West as a place—one that stretches westward from states on the 98th meridian (e.g., Texas, North Dakota) to states that border the Pacific Ocean; and multiracial relations, from Afro-Spanish explorer Esteban in 1528 to the present.

In the canon of Black New Mexico scholarship, *Blackdom* differs from what has been written, which up to 2023 has been very little. The first notable written work was in 1976 by Barbara Richardson, author of *Black Directory of New Mexico*. It would not be until 2004 that another book would critically address the history of Blacks in New Mexico in Maisha Baton's oral history *Do Remember Me* (2004). Between the writing of these two works there had been a plethora of local histories written by New Mexicans who had little historical training. A few publications written by trained historians focused on the Black frontier; they included articles on Esteban and the freedom-seeking mulatta Isabel de Olvera as well as several books on Buffalo Soldier Second Lieutenant Henry O. Flipper. In the 2010s, works like Bruce Glasrud's (ed.) *African American History in New Mexico: Portraits from Five Hundred Years* (2013) and Randolph Stakeman's book chapter, "African Americans in Albuquerque, 1880–1930: A Demographic Analysis" in Herbert G. Ruffin II and Dwayne A. Mack (eds.) *Freedom's Racial Frontier: African Americans in the Twentieth-Century West* (2018) extended Black New Mexico's history into the domain of contemporary western scholarship. As a modern frontier history that follows the path blazed by Kenneth Wiggins Porter and Sherman Savage but is also focused on twentieth-century developments, *Blackdom* continues along the contemporary western trajectory as a history of significance about African Americans in the rural West.

To date, Black New Mexico's history is dominated by work on African Americans in Albuquerque. In the early twentieth century, this town was an agricultural community that transitioned into a commercial city with a small industrial core. At that time, Albuquerque's black community was small, isolated, and made up mostly of a people relegated to labor as cooks, domestics, and service workers who had migrated to New Mexico on the Santa Fe railroad from Texas and the Deep South. Like other black westerners, they were active in their pursuit for freedom, forming black institutions, including churches, stores, self-help organizations, and a National Association for the Advancement of Colored People (NAACP) chapter to fight racial segregation in education and public accommodations. This experience differed from that in the southeastern section of the state, where Blackdom and Chaves County stood. During the early twentieth century, much of the latter area was known as "Little Texas" in part due to its oil production and large population of white Texans who eventually required statehood and a shift to local power, institutionalizing Jim Crow into the region after New Mexico gained statehood. As for Black migrants, this was a place where Black military men and Black farmers settled. They built a parallel community and economy that relied on its Black community—which was not the case in Albuquerque. More significant is the difference in that through corporate oil drilling, Blackdomites thrived in the 1920s, the same period in which African Americans in other parts of New Mexico stagnated socioeconomically. Outside of studies on the Roswell Correctional Center, this area has received scant historical attention. The few histories of Black New Mexicans tend to focus on their urban experiences during the Second Great Migration (1940–1970) highlighted by civil rights activism and a population that grew from 4,672 in 1940 to 19,555 in 1970.

Having observed this project grow from post-dissertation development to book, I found the history's connection to my research and to my own father's family history in freedmen settlements in Seguin, Texas, to be of great interest. And I have learned that through land ownership, critical planning, and faith, Black families and groups like the Blackdom Townsite Company always had the potential to build what Nelson calls an "Afrotopia" or African American utopian community. Similar to places explored in *Black Towns and Profit*, Blackdom was unique in that it was forged by African Americans as both a refuge from Jim Crow and as a place for Black economic empowerment. It evolved from dry farming and Black survival (from 1903 to ca. 1922) to black landowners receiving royalty checks from corporate oil drilling and to their thriving until the Great Depression; and, possibly beyond, according to Frank Boyer (1st Blackdom Townsite Company President). As a history, *Blackdom* differs from the histories of African America and the African American West, not because the racially regenerative quest to forge a "Promised Land" has never been attempted but because the intentional development of an Afrotopia was accomplished in the most unlikely of places and times, in New Mexico and during Blacks' radical transformation and embracing of urban-industrial life during their Great Migration. This focus and interconnecting of Borderlands history with the interdisciplinary-transdisciplinary nature of Africana scholarship gives *Blackdom* the potential to be the model for our understanding of Black Town formation and function in the twenty-first century.

HERBERT G. RUFFIN II, ASSOCIATE PROFESSOR
SYRACUSE UNIVERSITY, ARTS & SCIENCES,
AFRICAN AMERICAN STUDIES

Syracuse, New York
January 3, 2023

PREFACE

Blackdom was a real place. I have to make this fact clear because my brother Maison Nelson thought I made it up. No lie. Maison (pronounced May Sawn) recorded my doctoral graduation on December 10, 2015. He flew all the way from the Air Force base where he was stationed in Las Vegas, Nevada, to El Paso, Texas. He took pictures of me holding my University of Texas at El Paso mock diploma (a degree in Borderland History with subfield expertise in African Diasporic Studies and US History). Yet, after my not seeing him for about five years, Maison's question was, "When you gon' make some money?"

In 2019, I accepted a seat on a panel at the national conference for the Western History Association in Las Vegas, Nevada, held at the Westgate Vegas Resort & Casino, near the Vegas Strip. Dr. Kenneth Hamilton was on the panel, and I could not pass up the chance to meet him in person. Unknown to Dr. Hamilton, he had become an intellectual father to the Blackdom Thesis and an all-around icon for me. Maison drove from his house in the Northside of Vegas to meet me at the conference. At first sight, again, "When you gon' make some money?" Forgive me for belaboring the point, but Blackdom was a real place. Audible to the people sitting around Maison in the conference room of my panel, he said, "Oh. I thought he made that up."

University of Texas at El Paso Graduation, December 10, 2015. Courtesy of the author.

OFFICIAL REPLACEMENTS FOR THE OLD PUBLIC BLACKDOM NARRATIVES

Blackdom Townsite and Company (1900–1930): A Brief History

In the early 1900s, the Pecos Valley Region of Southeastern New Mexico Territory experienced an economic boom because of an influx of settlers into the area. African American families were among those settlers. They built Blackdom, the only all-Black town in the territory and situated it about twenty miles south of Roswell in Chaves County. Today little remains of this ambitious frontier scheme that within a twenty-year period became an oil producing town.

In September 1903, thirteen black men led by Isaac W. Jones and Francis M. (Frank) Boyer, signed the Articles of Incorporation to establish the Blackdom Townsite Company to build the town. Blackdom was located on a direct route to the Dexter train station to the East, and Artesia, another New Mexico Territory boomtown twenty miles south. West of Blackdom was Apache land.

A few of the early founders were former soldiers in the all-Black 24th Infantry which served throughout New Mexico Territory in the 1880s and 1890s. Frank Boyer was the most influential of them having trained as a minister at Atlanta (Georgia) Baptist College (now Morehouse College) following his discharge from the military. Boyer and his wife, Ella, also brought black Freemasonry to the county establishing the first Masonic lodge in 1914. A frontier town relying on dry farming proved difficult to maintain. Survival depended on rain that often didn't come. Between 1909 and 1916, however, the rains came and Blackdom was prosperous. In 1917, Blackdom saw many of its young men conscripted into the military as the US entered World War I.

When oil was discovered in 1919, Blackdom residents created the Blackdom Oil Company. The single largest investor, however, was Mittie Moore Wilson, an African American brothel owner in nearby Roswell. Blackdom Oil contracted with the New York–based National Exploration Company to drill wells in the area. Current research doesn't provide exact numbers of working wells, but a 1947 interview with Frank Boyer revealed that some Blackdom residents still received royalties from Gulf Oil for producing wells on their property.

Frank Boyer in a 1947 interview recalled a peak of about 800 black residents in the town and surrounding township in the early 1920s. US Census records, however, revealed that only 400 African Americans lived in Blackdom and Chaves County by 1930. Many of those residents owned a home in town and a desert homestead (ranch). Others resided exclusively outside the town limits. In fact, town leaders ran ads in state and national newspapers and *The Crisis* magazine that said: "farmers preferred."

In 1927, the town gathered and celebrated Juneteenth, where they hosted their white neighbors with a baseball game and barbecue. Despite the continuing oil revenues for some residents, the 1929 Stock Market Crash and Great Depression effectively ended Blackdom's future as an independent town. Town leaders dissolved Blackdom in 1930.

Blackdom Oil Company (1919–1930): A Brief History

In 1919, ironically, Blackdom Oil Company started during Red Summer in a year of nationwide violence against Black people. Blackdom was New Mexico's only all-Black town that entered contracts with National Exploration Company and Mescalero Oil Company. Oil exploration began in Southeastern New Mexico during the 1910s earning the region the nickname "Little Texas." Commercialization allowed Blackdom to fully engage the regional economy during the Roaring Twenties.

Oil was first discovered in New Mexico in 1907 and commercial wells began in 1922. In 1919, Blackdomites benefited from the speculation bubble when the homestead class incorporated the Blackdom Oil Company. Leaders in the collective were led by engineers and Freemasons of prominent families (Boyer, Ragsdale, Eubank, Gates, and Collins, to name a few) who agreed to deposit their land with the Roswell Picacho Investment Co. at a bank twenty miles North.

Blackdom had begun in September 1903 when thirteen African American men, led by Isaac Jones and Frank Boyer, incorporated the townsite company. The early years were plagued with droughts in a dry-farming agricultural society. By 1918, for those slow to prove up land, prospects for an oil boom in the region increased urgency. Women of Blackdom increased their land holdings, led by Ella Boyer, who completed her 160-acre patent on land adjacent to Blackdom's forty-acre townsite (land patented by her husband Frank).

The year 1919 saw the first significant African American participation in the region's oil boom. In September of that year, Mittie Moore Wilson homesteaded a square mile of land three miles south of Blackdom. She struggled to meet proving up requirements until she received help from a few influential people of the town. Moore, a bootlegger who ran a house of prostitution twenty miles north of the town, was one of the area's wealthiest citizens.

In January 1920, Blackdomites placed a "Will Drill at Blackdom" announcement in the *Roswell Daily Record*, inviting wildcatters and other oil speculators to participate in the boom that promised riches for Blackdomites who had lands made available for oil drilling. The fury of advertisements for Blackdom Oil peaked in the summer that year as local residents signed contracts with oil exploration companies from New York to California. On September 1, 1920, The *Roswell Daily Record* reported an unidentified California syndicate had, "Made Location at Blackdom." How many wells and barrels produced by Blackdom's enterprise is currently lost to history.

Lasting prosperity materialized in Blackdom's outposts that were sustained by inter-commerce amongst families within a vast regional network of Masonic lodges and churches. During the 1920s, the town itself withered even as Blackdomites in the region garnered oil royalties. Eustace and Francis Jr., of the Boyer family, were a part of a WWI cohort of military men who proved up homesteads during the postwar period and grew their families. Committed to an Afrotopia underwritten by oil royalties, Frank Boyer left Chaves County, where

Blackdom was located, and resettled in Vado, Doña Ana County, New Mexico after completing the townsite's official plat in May of 1920. Following the departure, the Ragsdale family maintained an influence through their business dealings in windmills as well as oil pumping on their land.

By 1930 and the start of the Great Depression, Blackdom's townsite ceased to exist. Blackdom Oil, however, continued to produce royalties for the homestead class. Local newspapers reported that the Blackdom Oil Company drilled exploration wells at least 1,600 feet deep. Frank Boyer, in a 1947 interview, said that royalty payments to Blackdomites flowed well into the post–World War II era.

ACKNOWLEDGMENTS

This book is an attempt to fully articulate ideas developed in my 2015 dissertation. For this reason, and seven years later, the person principally responsible for the full development of the Afro-Frontier thesis is Marissa Renee Roybal. After graduation, I was hoping to forget about Blackdom and move on. However, I couldn't find a job or a project worth the time and energy spent. When Marissa Roybal summoned her entrepreneurial spirit, Blackdom Townsite Company had life once more and the Afro-Frontier thesis had a rebirth in September 2019. Marissa cultivated an institution from a dissertation and an idea to produce this refined study of Blackdom, New Mexico. Brilliant.

INTELLECTUAL TECHNOLOGY

THOUGHT PROCESS, TERMINOLOGY, AND TRANSLITERATIONS

At the turn of the twentieth century, African descendant peoples refused to participate in the perpetual smoldering of their dehumanization and made choices to segregate themselves behind the corporate veil of municipality. Few outlets exist to explore the conscious efforts of African descendants who sought autonomy through notions of God and regenerative agricultural practices in frontier spaces. If not distracted by the minstrel-like "Blackness" in popular media, consciously, one may find significance in "Black" sovereignty that extended beyond notions of a fragile freedom. Undergirding the historical significance of "Black" bodies in the Borderlands, Blackdomites struck oil in the 1920s. Finding Blackdom oil was significant because Blackdom ascended to Afrotopia.

Borderland Studies helps to inform this new Black history. This narrative contains remixed "intellectual technology" to help the reader better absorb the methods, breadth, and scope used to reintroduce a story to people who thought they knew "Blackdom" and introduce a narrative to people who have never heard of Blackdom. In an effort to override a systematically imposed ignorance blanketing the United States and the world, I intentionally quarantine a reader to focus on the material presented.

"Black People" was a notion developed by those attempting to craft a narrative of "White" superiority as well as project the normalcy of "White" supremacy using popular media. As Europeans sought to colonize Indigenous places and spaces, they created creature-like cognitive relationships between skin color, labor, and personhood. The history of "Whiteness" reveals an association between the desired signifier of "White" people as the antithesis of "Black" people. The manufacture of "Blackness" in popular media has distorted reality for people of African descent and the identities they subscribed to.

For a more cogent reading of my work, below I define "Black" and all the major corresponding derivatives due to the mass production as well as commodification of "Blackness" in popular culture. Due in part to the soul murder of some Black folks, this book contains material that may appear foreign.

Black, when referencing people of African descent, refers to the intersection of people and politics.

Blackness embodies the constant morphosis of border-dweller bodies, politics, and the existential crisis of "White" hegemonic power.

Black people, the term, embraces the humanity of people under the condition of "Americanism."

Black sovereignty articulates the exercise of freedom within the "Souls of Black Folk" and the existential manifestations.

Blackdom Townsite Company enabled Black People to reach sovereignty in a legal system designed to assure "White" hegemonic power.

Blackdom, as a term, functions as a catch-all expression with some focus on place.

"Blackdom" has an emphasis on space rather than place for the purpose of including intangible signified notions of Black People.

Blackdomite imbues the bold possession of Black Sovereignty and brands those who engaged in "Blackdom."

Black colonizer refers to a distinctive experience of Black folks' centuries-long colonization effort and distinguishes between other colonizing forces that invaded Indigenous lands.

Black cowboy identifies and emphasizes an often untold, mostly unknown, and/or misrepresentation of Black People who engaged "The West." In this narrative, Black cowboy culture refers to a distinct culture, rather than popular projections of "Cowboying."

Black consciousness sheathes the intellectual infrastructure of collective notions understood by people under the conditions of American Blackness.

Black colonization continuum assumes the ontology of Black folks' functions across generations as a guiding light to freedom and sovereignty.

Black ministers nurtured the sovereignty impulse of Black folks throughout the Black colonization continuum.

Black military personnel commanded respect in such a way that they helped shift and shape an often "illiterate," yet wise, community.

Black Freemasons were an outgrowth of Black folks' striving and a signature institution in part responsible for Black folks' cognitive and multidimensional engagement of Mexico's northern frontier.

If the Black colonization continuum had a destination from its messianic trajectory, Afrotopia explains the manner in which "Black" people existed in diaspora. Moreover, the standardization of their archetypal course of striving demonstrates their cognitive adaptability to learn from the past and replicate a prosperous present. Afro-Frontier defines a specific course for "Blackdomites," who adapted in Mexico's northern frontier, "frontier" space White colonizers stole from Native and Indigenous peoples. Afro-Frontierists were opportunists and beneficiaries in an era of "American frontierism." Blackdom was a microcosm of hegemonic society: separate-but-equal.

Afro-Frontierism unifies the thought process above. Afrocentric notions of utopia often hinge on a mythologized trajectory of victimhood and or redemption. Most often, "promised land" functions as an invocation of physical space divinely prepared for the faithful. In this narrative, Blackdom was both "promised land" and "promised (government) lands" confiscated from Indigenous peoples.

My intent is to be respectful of this era's skepticism of experts. Considering all known information can be accessed with a touch of a screen in the palm of your hands, misinformation also exists in the same space. Often reconciling competing narratives works to the advantage of hegemonic society, and I do not desire to further distract the reader. For example, throughout this piece, I consent to using "Black" when referencing people of African descent; even though race does not exist, racism does. Although "Black" was a Europeanized bastardization of Africanity, through a refined process of struggle, "Black people" wrestled with the colonization, and we must do the same.

BLACKDOM, NEW MEXICO

INTRODUCTION

On September 1, 1920, the *Roswell Daily Record* reported, "Blackdom Location Made":

> The location for the deep test well at Blackdom south of this city has just been made. This well will be drilled a quarter of a mile west of Blackdom and the derrick is now under construction. The well will be put down by a California syndicate represented here by Verne Lincoln. A Rotary rig will be used to go the first 1,000 feet and excellent progress is expected.[1]

BLACKDOM, BLACKDOMITES, AND AFRO-FRONTIERISM

Blackdom

My mother, Veretha, and I started out in Los Angeles, California, during the late 1970s. Around the age of five, I went to live with my grandparents in Compton, California. My grandfather, Glenorce, as well as my father, Timothy, were born in Lott, Texas. Daddy Glen found the rural railroad town lacking, compared to his dreams. Like many Black cowboys, he used the military to escape; he served in the Navy during the Korean conflict, although he never saw war up close. Daddy Glen traded (in) his rural life for the big cities on the West Coast of America. After three years, he went back to Lott and reunited with his young family before they headed to San Pedro, California. Daddy Glen's appreciation for the ocean view was, in part, why he chose Harbor City to start a new life.

Mary Elizabeth (Gilmore) Nelson of Lott, Daddy Glen's wife, was ready to leave her rustic beginnings behind, and they focused on a more metropolitan future together. After a short time renting in West Coast port cities, the Nelson family bought a house in Compton, California. During the 1970s, the Nelson family ballooned to eight kids (five sons, three daughters). Today, the two are still married, living in the same family home. While they traded in their rural life for the inner city, they continued to return to Texas for annual family reunions and owned property in Lott, and my granddad never stopped wearing his Black Boots.

During the uprising of 2020, the mainstream of America was illuminated by the existence of "Black cowboys" who resided in cities across the United States. In a summer of protest, the *New York Times* took note of Black people on horseback in support of anti-racist protesters with the headline, "Evoking History, Black Cowboys Take to the Streets."[2] For many people, Compton was known to have a "cowboy" culture, but rarely was popular culture exposed to Black "Urban" Cowboys and Cowgirls on horses from the hub city. Once popular culture has caught up, soon there will be a crowd to follow those who perform as if in a minstrel show. This book serves to preserve a less performative notion of "Black cowboying."

The offspring of people who developed Blackdom, Black Towns, and Black enclaves took root in inner cities at the beginning of the twentieth century and bore fruit in the twenty-first. Black folks from Black enclaves, colonies, and incorporated all-Black towns increased their concentration in American cities during World War I, and populations accelerated into the World War II era. Rural and small-town Black folks filtered into urban areas with formal training and income and began to build families. Inner-city population growth correlated with the depopulation of autonomous Black spaces. The influx of "Black cowboys" and rural people enforced the transition of urban life through the development of micro socioeconomic markets. Echoed in popular culture, Black bodies and talents were a source of generational wealth creation, if exploited.

Notions of Blackness have rarely included the dynamism of Black cowboy culture. Although now evident in the paper of record, Black cowboys exist in inner cities across the United States. Within the hidden history of "freedom colonies," Black Towns, and other Black community intersections, we explore a history of Black ambitions. As they transported themselves into the Borderlands, they developed in a "cowboy culture." However, few might see themselves through the popular notion of "cowboy." "Cowboying" was only part of Black folks' alchemical process in frontier spaces as they quickly adjusted and adapted, a signature of their culture of thriving.

Black cowboy culture was much more than that which one could see, and the brilliance was often buried in the mundanity of documents. Black people on horseback who were cowboys and cowgirls show the clear connection between Black cowboys and the standard "cowboy" narrative. This study extends beyond the perfunctory and descends into the conscience of Black folks who engaged in Afrotopia. Part of Black cowboy culture was the dignity of understated elegance. For example, Daddy Glen wore a Jheri curl (when it was stylish) and never stopped wearing his Black cowboy boots. Arguably, processed hair was far from an understatement. However, the shine of his hair mirrored the shine on his boots in recognition of his feet, grounded in his (Nelsonian) cowboy culture.

This book begins a new dialectic to better explore and understand Black cowboy culture. In a 2018 recorded interview with Albuquerque, New Mexico, KOAT 7 Action News's Kay Dimanche, the latter asked,

"So, what is Blackdom?" I replied, "It was an investment vehicle." Consistently, my responses in the interview did not easily translate into "action" or "news," and the interview did not air. "Blackdomites struck oil!" I should have exclaimed when I realized how poorly the interview was going.

I knew that "Blackdom" was understood as a "Negro refuge" that started around 1900, and that term was what one might expect to hear after the question was asked. However, I had recently discovered Blackdom's lost years as an oil company. My discovery was that of a new Blackdom that changed the course of New Mexico's history: Black people who had invested in a "township" at the start of the twentieth century entered the Roaring Twenties as part of a solely Black-owned oil company. "Blackdom" allowed people under the conditions of American Blackness (Black people) to fully invest in themselves without the impositions of others. Blackdom, New Mexico, "was a real place with a little magic," is what I should have said.

The excavation of "Blackdom" has the ability to help retell Black history in the twentieth century as the multitudes grapple with hidden histories and their fruits: specifically, Black cowboys. So little has been done on the topic that the term suggests Black people are a part of the American Cowboy culture. As the history of Black cowboy culture filters into the popular imagination, one must wrestle with notions of westward expansion, the West, and other articulations that describe confiscated Indigenous lands that help promote the notions of White supremacy and Manifest Destiny.[3] A vast majority of popular culture cowboys are shown as White people on horseback. The current revelation of Black cowboys in American cities does not negate that they were there the whole time. Instead, their presence reflects a need for new history and understanding to fully grasp their significance.

After Blackdom's demise during the Dust Bowl (1930s), a host of incorporated Black towns fell victim to the era of dryness. Blackdomites, and Black rural folks in frontier spaces did not wither with the crops; they continued to migrate. More importantly, the ideas of "Blackdom" traveled with them. In Chaves County, the people who fully invested in Blackdom were in a fairer economic condition than most due to capital appreciation and the oil company. Most Blackdomites, because of royalties from leased Blackdom land, were well positioned to weather the famine that came. Migration out of "Blackdom" was expected and planned. Many children of Blackdom matured and resumed the ancestral search for opportunity and generational wealth or looked to preserve capital. In the inner cities of Seattle, Compton, Oakland, Detroit, Houston, Dallas, Chicago, Philadelphia, and across what became the United States of America, Black cowboy children became inhabitants.

Blackdomites

"Blackdomites Struck Oil!" On September 1, 1920, a California-based oil exploration syndicate contracted with Blackdom Oil Company and "made location." Similar to the town, the oil company was owned entirely by Black folks. "Blackdom" transitioned into a place where investors in the township received royalty payments for leasing land to oil extraction companies. The new orientation of Blackdomite society shifted town business from a regenerative homesteader agricultural context to a more extractive-oriented concept. Previous historians of Blackdom's history misunderstood the societal shift. In early narratives about Blackdom, the 1920s was a time of abandonment. This history of "Blackdom" narrates a time of documented abundance.

Blackdomites were believers and doers in "Blackdom." Landholding Blackdomites received royalty payments into the post–WWII period, decades after the town became uninhabited.[4] This Blackdom narrative includes a lost history of generational wealth and Afrotopia as well as Blackdomite possession of "Promised [government] Land." Presumably, the people of "Blackdom" did not refer to themselves as "Blackdomites." The term therefore describes the conscious intersection of people engaging in "Blackdom." Confirmation of royalty payments from the Blackdom scheme suggests forethought. Analysis of Blackdomite society begins to reconcile the old Blackdom narrative with the new.

The Roswell Correctional Center, which currently sits on Blackdom land, is a visual reminder that helps to conceal the dynamism of the all-Black town. Arguably, inmates who inhabit what was Blackdom might be considered Blackdomites because of their current location. However, Blackdomite implies a conscious engagement of "Blackdom." Over time, Blackdom methods of expression and tactics changed. Most vivid was the decreased physical occupation of Blackdom during the 1920s juxtaposed with the exponential growth in land mass after Blackdomites "struck oil." No previous Blackdom narrative has explored the implications of Blackdom Oil Company and the impact on Blackdom and "Blackdomites."

Afro-Frontierism

Reconstructing Blackdom's newly discovered history required a wider view and a new lens to fully see significance in the mundanity of documents. Development of the Afro-Frontier notion was a way to define this intersection of Black people in the Borderlands. Dr. Kenneth Hamilton, best known for his work *Black Towns and Profit*, might argue that one was "making things up."[5] Dr. Hamilton made a similar remark in reference to the "new" ways of doing history using theory and frameworks to "re-imagine." Between sessions at the 2019 Western History Association conference, I asked Dr. Hamilton how he saw the "profit motive" in the development of Black Towns when others couldn't. He said, "It was in the documents." Blackdom Oil Company was in the documents.

Intentionally or unintentionally, popular historical frameworks, theories, and narratives purport that Black people in general, and the town of Blackdom, specifically, had little capacity or ability to construct an oil-producing town during the Roaring Twenties. To augment the lack of imagination about Black folks in general, and Black towns specifically, this study adopts the Black colonization continuum framework to highlight the long-held impulse of African descendants to migrate and colonize, as part of their "hustle."[6]

Blackdomites Struck Oil! The establishment of Blackdom Oil Company was in the documents. However, the State of New Mexico's Centennial-approved account of the Blackdom narrative mentions nothing about Blackdom Oil or Blackdomites during the 1920s. A popular representation of Blackdom continues to suggests the town was abandoned in the mid-1920s. Blackdom Oil Company was far from a mundane discovery in the documents, but the new information was hard to reconcile with Blackdom's public standard narrative trajectory that implied fecklessness and failure rather than forethought.

CHAPTER BREAKDOWN

Epistemologically, this book supports the idea that captured in the subaltern histories of African descendants, although often untold, there existed an omnipresent collective consciousness to "colonize." Transfixed on the history of early Black "American" institutional intersections of African descendant ministers, military personnel, and Freemasons, one identifies a pattern of autonomy projects as a through-line in US history. Informed by the Blackdom thesis, colonization was a product of "Black" consciousness: intersectional Blackness. Black colonization was proactive, and over time Black folks perfected migration and colonization by building Black institutions over hundreds of years.

The anecdotal narrative throughout this book invites readers to find themselves in Blackdom's history. Modeled in microcosmic moments, my life growing up in Compton illustrated the continuum. Informed by my life story and recognition of Black cowboy culture, readers have the option to reimagine notions of "inner city" Blackness. As the twenty-first century begins similarly to the twentieth century, it is important to reexamine historical analyses of the past. For example, I found Blackdom Oil Company due to the power of this digitized age of historical research. However, I had few modern ways to analyze the new data.

Tonally, this work amplifies skepticism about what consumers of this work were taught about "Blackness." In chapter 1, "Boyer, Blackdom

Colonization, and Continuum," Frank Boyer's life trajectory as a Buffalo Soldier (military), minister, and Freemason underscores the Blackdomite institutional intersection with Mexico's northern frontier. Frank was Blackdom Townsite Company's first president and was one major figure among thirteen Black men who signed the articles of incorporation. Evident in townsite company documents, early Blackdomites shared influences. Significant to Boyer and Blackdom's history, African descendant communities of people who nurtured ministers, military personnel, and Freemasons agitated autonomy projects with colonization outcomes starting in the late 1700s and into Blackdom (1903–1930).

Intentionally, Blackdomites benefited from an early cohort of Black folks who engaged a Spanish-speaking Borderland in the pursuit of Afrotopia as the space transitioned into a US western territory.[7] Ambitious Black folks sought opportunity in Chaves County in the US territory of New Mexico. Chapter 2, "Preconditions," describes the major economic drivers of regional markets that encouraged Black colonization. Frank Boyer's life functions as a testament to the legacy of Black intersectional institutions that protected Black folks from hegemonic societal damnation. Blackdom in the Borderlands was a bold regional phenomenon, where Black people veiled their ambitions in barren Indigenous blood-soaked lands and "Blackness."[8]

The narrative impulse to mythologize a unique figure competes with the inclusion of the thirteen co-founders of Blackdom Townsite Company and asks that one explore "Blackdom." A broader understanding of the collective toil allows one to visualize a community in motion, rather than see a single Moses-like figure directing Blackdom's narrative. Behind the corporate veil of Blackdom Townsite Company, Black folks engaged the world as frontier sovereigns. The Blackdom Thirteen were all influenced by Black institutions that helped them consciously commune with one another.

In "Prophets, Profits, and the Proffit Family" (chapter 3), the reader is introduced individually to the Blackdom Thirteen in the order of official dates on their homestead patent as well as to those who didn't homestead. Blackdomites sought Afrotopia and achieved it within a twenty-year period, appearing as though Blackdom was prophetic of an arrival into a "promised land." Blackdom existed as a townsite frontier scheme; however, the lives of Blackdomites do not reflect the dynamism of their strivings. The seemingly simple lives of Black folks in Chaves County produced profits. Encapsulated in the brief synopsis of the Proffit family legacy, one begins to witness the power of "Blackdom" worthy of illumination.

The public documentation of Blackdom revealed elements of the prophetic, humble lives of prophets, and tangible profits. At a simple intersection they began a conversation about utopia. The first of a three-part series on Afrotopia in Chaves County, chapter 4 discloses a biblical consciousness that existed in Blackdomites. Their faith was on display. For three decades, Blackdom was a purpose-driven space that provided Black folks the environment to thrive. In every decade following the incorporation of the Blackdom Townsite Company there was a consistent renewal of faith. Although 1903 to 1909 were considered Blackdom's "lost years," faith surmounted failure as Black homesteaders endured drought and social transition. Survival into a time of revival was a measure of "success."

Chapter 5 consists of two parts and continues a theme of duality in the lives of Black women. Conscious of not "speaking for" Black women, I lend my privilege to highlight a silent space often overlooked. Silent spaces, 100 years ago in Blackdom, remain silent; however, Black women's public record informs the trajectory of the two-part series. The first half explores Ella Boyer's public record and the archetypal life of Blackdomite women of faith as well as their affinity to institutionalize. The public and infamous life of Mattie (Mittie) Moore Wilson shapes the second half of the chapter to highlight her conscious intersections with institutions. Black women built power and fueled Revival Times into Boom Times. This new Blackdom narrative suggests that women were significant and fortified both the township and the oil company.

Chapter 6 introduces new Black history discovered over the course of conducting research into Blackdom's public record. Frequent references are made to articles published during the time, supporting this new Black history. The unearthing of the Blackdom Oil Company suggests a greater importance of Black bodies as well as Black consciousness in the "development" of the southeastern section of the US territory of New Mexico. The popular history of New Mexico—a region organized as a tricultural society—suggests Black people were insignificant. Blackdom was a microcosm of hegemonic society that supports a more complicated narrative. Further Chapter 7 is a postscript and a veiled call to action.

CHAPTER 1

BOYER, BLACKDOM COLONIZATION, AND CONTINUUM

If there was one person whose life encapsulated Blackdomite society and the Afro-Frontier, it was Francis (Frank) Marion Boyer, the quintessential archetype of Black military, ministers, and Freemasons. Frank's real life was dynamic, but popular stories about him mythologizes Blackdom and borrows from only part of his story. Leaving little room for historical analysis or imagination, Frank was often introduced as the leader of Blackdom, New Mexico. In this study, Frank was recognized as one of many leaders in Blackdomite society who were trained thinkers and doers. In the 1890s, Frank first entered Mexico's northern frontier as part of the 24th Infantry (Buffalo

Soldiers). His unit functioned as border patrol. Black military personnel had authority and tremendous autonomy in the Borderlands. Buffalo Soldiers were a vital element in the US exploitation of Indigenous peoples and enforced the annexation of their lands.

After Frank's military service ended in the early 1890s, he returned to Georgia where he attended Atlanta Baptist College (Morehouse College today) and trained as a minister. He was an active member of his local Prince Hall Freemason lodge before returning to the Borderlands. In the Pecos River Valley, Frank executed his Afrotopic plans. Mythmaking has a place, but Frank's real life helps reveal intersections that invited Black migrants to conceive of Afrotopia with him. At the turn of the twentieth century, some Black institutions grew into multimillion-dollar enterprises. Blackdom was the latest scheme with a business plan to harness the power of people who embraced hard work and who trained as ministers, military personnel, and Freemasons. Anomalous as building a town on desert prairies seemed, Blackdom was the only incorporated all-Black town in the Territory of New Mexico, which became a state in 1912, during Blackdom's revival.

TERRITORY OF NEW MEXICO

Today little remains of the scheme that began September 5, 1903, although Frank Boyer maintained that Blackdom Oil produced royalty payments into the post–World War II era.[1] The Blackdom scheme was led by minister Francis M. Boyer (president), Reverend Isaac W. Jones (vice president), Professor Daniel G. Keys (secretary), and Burrel Dickerson (treasurer), along with nine other Black men who signed Blackdom Townsite Company's Articles of Incorporation.[2] Blackdom Townsite Company was the institution organized by Black people to build a town named Blackdom. Blackdomites related themselves according to defined ideas and ideals evident in their documented articulations of self-governance.

Rightly, many authors focus attention on Blackdom's co-founder and first president, Frank Boyer. Important to this study, however, we focus on where Black migrants engaged Frank to better understand Blackdom as more than a place that came and went. Blackdom was a proof of concept for ambitious, intentional, intellectual Black folks who nurtured frontier sovereignty. For example, predictably, Isaac was a minister; and, like Frank, he approached life with a messianic zeal. Isaac was the first in the company to homestead for Blackdom in the spring of 1903. In Chaves County, Blackdom became a real place when Frank completed a forty-acre homestead patent for Township 13S - Range 24E Aliquots NE 1/4 SE 1/4 Sections 26 on July 10, 1914.[3] The town square was located about five miles on a direct route west of the Dexter train station. Artesia was twenty miles south and Roswell was twenty miles north, both towns of which were linked by Highway 285. All the divisions into villages, towns, and cities in Chaves County were originally Mescalero Apache land.

This study begins on biblically dry silt and sand, where Black folks employed colonizer freedoms in pursuit of frontier sovereignty. Histories and folklore about the impact of major/minor US slave institutions often overshadow the perpetual story of ambitious diasporic African descendants. This excavation of Black migration/colonization ascribes meaning to patterns consistent in Black folks' striving and includes slavery as one of many conditions under American Blackness. Current propagation of America's grand narratives precludes a popular acknowledgment of Black bodies in the Spanish Borderlands as significant. Specifically, the grand narrative of New Mexico promotes a "tricultural" (Indigenous, Spanish, and White) narrative that subsequently prosecutes an exclusionary argument.

Moreover, Black warriors have always been essential characters in Afrocentric grand narratives. During the US annexation of Mexico's northern frontier in the second half of the nineteenth century, Black military personnel proved useful in the region's transmogrification of Mexico's northern frontier into US territory. Buffalo Soldiers helped position Black people to benefit in the contestation of stolen lands. Acknowledgment of Black people in military service provides evidence for significance in Black people's engagement of the US–Mexico Borderlands. Although few in number, Black people were fundamental to the US westward expansion efforts and had an outsized influence. The Blackdom community reflected the larger hegemonic society and represented a microcosm of colonizer intentionality. Echoing colonization efforts, Blackdom was a transcolonial model of the hegemonic society.

The extraction of meaning from conscious/documented efforts on the part of Blackdomites reveals a macro-Afrocentric colonization continuum that often began in desert frontiers. Migration and colonization cycles echoed throughout African diasporic histories. This study suggests migration/colonization patterns congealed in the micro-event of the Blackdom Townsite Company's incorporation. Blackdom was the latest manifestation of inherited Afrocentric intentionality. Sovereignty ideas traveled as African bodies jostled through the Middle Passage of the trans-Atlantic slave trade and into slave institutions.

The existential crisis of slavery and American Blackness propagated by major/minor institutions did little to deter an ancestral striving to employ freedoms in the manufacture of sovereign spaces. Institutionalized hegemonic pressure solidified communities of African descendants and transformed Africanity into a singular intersectional Blackness that produced a Black colonizer lens/perspective. In the mid-1800s, African descendants morphed into Black people who deliberately sought pathways to transition from free peoples to frontier sovereigns. Black community leaders were indifferent to integration and were often against burdening themselves with White impositions. The Blackdom experiment was a voluntary segregation that underwrote the sovereignty of Black folks.

Major slave institutions were defunct by 1865. Catalysts for migration varied from person to person, family to family, and congregation to congregation. Uniformly, self-determination and a conscious belief in sovereignty motivated Black migration/colonization schemes. Exoduster literature captured part of the intellectual dynamism employed by Black people. Exodusterism assumed Black people engaged the tangible world with a messianic zeal for a "promised land." Black institutions promoted Jewish and Christian as well as Muslim ideals and embossed biblical overtones that imbued Black folks to accept the demise of major slave institutions and pursue Afrotopic future sovereignty.

Unfortunately, mythologized narratives of Frank Boyer and Blackdom abound with little historical analysis. Frank's real life, instead, reflects a deeper history of Black colonizers. The burdens of American Blackness were too great to add migration to the condition based on reading an advertisement in a pamphlet or hearing about a colonization scheme from word of mouth. Black people, like Frank, needed more than a traumatic incident to push them to engage in Black colonization schemes.

At the intersection of Black ministers, Black military personnel, and Black Freemasonry, sovereignty strivings of Black folk were nurtured and achieved; such was the case for Blackdom. Blackdomite migration/colonization was born out of ancestral notions of sovereignty. Migration turbulence was difficult to endure without the skills of military personnel in the community and the compass of Freemasons in uncertain times. Communities of people under the conditions of American Blackness were nurtured in the three institutions that undergird a collective Afrotopic consciousness. Imbibed with the institutional knowledge, Black migration was a means, and sovereignty was the goal at the end. Ministers conditioned the people to view the world through the lens of God's sovereignty and Blackdom reflected an institutionalized daily, weekly, and monthly practice. Blackdomites were focused.

During the American Revolutionary War period, at the intersection of American Blackness, Black people developed Afro-subaltern responses to hegemonic society pressures. Prior to 1787, there were many African descendants who led colonization movements. The disruption of African ancestral knowledge of sovereignty was a result of the trans-Atlantic slave trade. In this study, African descendants substituted ancestral knowledge with institutionalized Afro-Abrahamic religious ideals. Ethiopianism manifested from the shared experience of Africans in diaspora and served as a replacement for lost ancestral knowledge. Collectively, Africans who transformed into Black people maintained religious notions that all magnified an undercurrent of divine sovereignty. For example, Black people in the late 1780s institutionalized Black liberation theology and sovereignty sentiments produced the African Methodist Episcopal (AME) Church and Bishop Richard Allen. In the same period, Prince Hall led a group of Black men in the creation of Freemason African lodges. Autonomy sentiments localized into conditions in which to achieve sovereignty.

Blackdom culminated a century of Black institutional refinement of liberation projects. Over the course of the nineteenth century, Black people perfected migration/colonization infrastructure to carry out Afrotopic destinies as an enterprise. Predictably, Black ministers, military personnel, and Freemasons led the Blackdom colonization scheme; the three institutions promoted the impulse for over a century. Black institutions nurtured Black spiritual and intellectual people. The revolutionary triad of ministers, military, and Freemasons helped formulate tangible and intangible measurements of one's humanity.

Blackdom Townsite Company's incorporation brought together the revolutionary triad of ambitious Black people who were transfixed on personal utopia, accounted for and measured by the standards of their religious beliefs. Although Blackdomites segregated themselves, they found opportunity. Black folks as "separate but equal" was the supreme law of the land after the 1896 *Plessy v. Ferguson* decision, which legalized racial segregation with the language of *Separate-but-Equal*. Now codified into law, Black bodies were finally equal rather than merely three-fifths human. "Black" people realized their ambitions in opportunity to be separate-*and*-equal under the law. When Blackdomites established the townsite company, only the land, water, and divine laws of sowing and reaping separated Black folks from Afrotopia. Some Black people who believed in God's sovereignty found solace in the legal doctrine. Black institutions taught the value of being separate, and equal in the legal sense. Many Black folks felt little need to be equal to people of a morally bankrupt society.

Black people in the US territory of New Mexico exploited their explicit sociolegal second-class citizenship after *Plessy*, combined with the territorial non-enforcement of Jim Crow laws. These two elements paved the way for Black people to take full advantage of their legal rights as citizens. Second-class citizenship was a privilege in the Borderlands, in part because it trumped non-citizenship. Religiously, Black people were conditioned to thrive in the background regardless of the condition in the foreground of their real lives. Blackdomites homesteaded on dry, drought-ridden desert prairies with a belief that the project would yield generational wealth.

Opening the homestead process with greater inclusion and opportunity for Black folks began the greatest bull market for colonization schemes in African diasporic history. The US annexation of Mexico's northern frontier transported Black colonizers into Westward expansion. Blackdom began in 1903, dissipated as a community around 1930, and continued to produce oil royalties into the post–World War II era. The significance of the successful autonomy experiment was the realized sovereignty. Developed by Black ministers, military men, and Freemasons, Blackdom became a real place where African descendants lived as sovereigns in tune with God's laws of divine seed time and harvest time.

THE CONTINUUM

As early as the seventh century BCE (25th Egyptian Dynasty), dark-skinned people formulated paths to realize God's sovereignty. In the story of Nubian warrior king Tirhakah, his ascendancy to Pharaoh began in military service. On his road to God's sovereignty, Tirhakah was first triumphant in battle, as he and his army traveled northward parallel to the Nile River, seizing power, both social and political, through occupation. Military victories earned him Egyptian social, political, and religious power. Recognizable Africanity was the relationship between sovereign spaces, military might, and the desire for a direct relationship with one's God(s). Embedded in the experience of African descendants was the migration/colonization relationship to military service in transition from colonized to colonizer/sovereign. For Black colonizers, the motivation to achieve God-like sovereignty was as potent a weapon as were the gunpowder-inspired weapons that developed in the seventeenth century.

In times of tumult and colonization, African descendants have consistently seized the opportunity to birth a new era for themselves, often through military service. In 1519, Juan Garrido (c. 1480 to c. 1550), a West African dark-skinned colonizer, became a wealthy landowner and wheat farmer after three decades of service to the Spanish Crown as part of colonization efforts in the sixteenth century. A Renaissance man living in Tenochtitlan or so-called "Mexico City," Juan embodied the global shift in ideological power from Islam to Christianity in pursuit of his Afrotopic yearning. Juan descended from Congolese people, and he converted from Islam when he traveled to Portugal. There, he adopted the Christian name Juan around 1490. While in Lisbon, he joined the Catholic Church as part of his transformation into a "conquistador." Juan took part in military campaigns at what became Puerto Rico and Cuba. His chief accomplishment was participation in toppling the Aztec capital at Tenochtitlan. Juan's trajectory mimicked a pattern of Africanity that extended back into antiquity.

The involuntary morphosis of Africanness into an American Blackness during the eighteenth century did little to erase notions of ancestral sovereignty. The institution of slavery blunted ancestral memory of African sovereignty. Ethiopianism as well as Black liberation theology bridged spiritual and cognitive gaps to propel ambitious Black folks to seek divine autonomy. Human ambitions persisted in the Afro-subaltern and surfaced as milestones along a continuum. The rise of Protestantism in the Great Awakening fed the instinct of African descendants to assume a direct and personal connection with their God(s). At the intersection of the American Revolution in the eighteenth century, African descendants carved new pathways to sovereignty through military service and incorporation. By the late 1700s, Black people collectively acted on their autonomy impulses.

MILITARY, MINISTERS, AND FREEMASONS

At the turn of the nineteenth century, Bishop Richard Allen led a Black "Great Awakening" during the post–Revolutionary era. Bishop Allen co-founded and led an autonomous sect of Episcopal Christians in development of a separate Black denomination incorporated as the African Methodist Episcopal (AME) Church.[4] In the wake of US independence from Britain, Black Freemasonry developed as an autonomy movement in service to African descendant peoples. Prince Hall Freemasonry, named for the leader of the Black liberationist movement, was made up of mostly military men. The church and Masonic military personnel became interdependent. Bishop Allen became a Prince Hall Freemason and Masonic military men joined the AME Church forming a synergistic intersectional Blackness. Prince Hall became a minister in Bishop Allen's AME Church and the perpetual motion machine of Black migration/colonization persisted with clear goals and measurements.

Afrotopic notions were planted early in fertile ground at the intersections of American Blackness and Ethiopianism. The infrastructure of the Black colonization networks nurtured relationships between military personnel, church folk, and Freemasons as they passed through frontier spaces. The growth in mutual aid societies during the American Revolution fostered various intellectual exchanges between ministers, military men, and Freemasons. African descendants projected an intentional Blackness with principles that fed sovereignty ambitions. For example, Paul Cuffee (January 17, 1759–September 7, 1817) was a minister from a Quaker society that supported his sense of Ethiopianism as an African descendant and agent of Black liberation. Cuffee spearheaded a back-to-Africa movement during his engagement with loyalists—Black people who chose military service to the British.

These loyalists, often referred to as the Ethiopian regiment, negotiated for the revocation of slavery in exchange for their military service. Those who survived the war were granted safe passage to live free in Nova Scotia, Canada, a British Black colonization scheme. Paul Cuffee lobbied and organized to help loyalists return to Africa and live out their Afrotopic dreams as colonizers on African soil in what became Sierra Leone, West Africa.

Consistent with Black activists of his day, Cuffee committed his effort to resurrect African civilization in the form of a pan-African "Christian" utopia. As a minister, Cuffee raised money and led lobbying efforts to encourage US abolitionists to push for repatriation of free Black folks to Africa in the British colony of Sierra Leone. His work in the American Colonization Society (ACS) helped establish Liberia in the 1820s; US officials decided not to work with British colonizers. In 1816, Cuffee's son Peter attended the First General Conference of the ACS in Philadelphia.

The ACS began as the American Society for Colonizing the Free People of Color in the United States before the group splintered as motivations shifted to building colonies for free Black people in West Africa. The society was first understood as an intersection for abolitionists and pro-slavers to agree; however, Black sovereignty notions were a threat to the system of slavery. People under the conditions of American Blackness transferred to sovereign spaces inspired revolution in ministers like Denmark Vesey.[5] At the intersection of ministers, military personnel, and Freemasons, Black people oriented themselves to realize God's sovereignty. Pro-slaver members such as Henry Clay denounced colonization efforts when they recognized the threat of Black people in slavery harboring to go beyond freedom in pursuit of their sovereignty notions.

Liberia had deep significance because it was a return to Africa and the fulfillment of an Afrotopic trajectory. Nell Painter, in her study of Black people migrating to Kansas to build Exoduster communities, found that over "ninety-eight thousand men, women and children enrolled on the emigration lists" signed up to go to Liberia in the 1860s.[6] The colony had become an independent nation in 1847.

Liberian diplomat Edward Blyden was at the center of global negotiations for a comprehensive pan-African agenda for both Sierra Leone (British colonization effort) and Liberia (United States colonization effort). In 1860, he wrote a letter to John Wilson, head of Foreign Missions of the Presbyterian Church Board in the United States, to ask that mission administrators reconsider their approach with Indigenous peoples. Liberia and the colonization efforts strained the relationship between the colonized Africans and African descendant colonizers. Nevertheless, in communities under the conditions of American Blackness, Liberia inspired hope for a sovereign future.

By the start of the US Civil War and the subsequent Emancipation Proclamation, Liberia's popularity began to languish and continued to decline in the decades that followed as Black people embraced a new era of "free-dom" in the United States. In an 1864 letter to President Abraham Lincoln, Edward Blyden asked that he encourage congressional action to fund emigration in support of repatriation. Although President Lincoln recognized the sovereignty of Liberia in 1862, he did not continue to support colonization.

Edward Blyden was the Liberian Secretary of State (1864–1866) and continued aggressive emigration lobby efforts. In 1867, Blyden explained the effect of having more investment and enterprising Black people in Liberia. He wrote:

> First, the various institutions of Liberia, political, religious, and educational are now in their forming state. We need models in each: something that the rising generation may see and have their aspirations kindled. The associations, whether physical or moral with which one is surrounded while obtaining his education have a great deal to do with the forming of one's character.[7]

Blyden continued to argue "Liberia as a means, not an end" and as "a child of divine providence."

Although Black people maintained a collective sovereignty consciousness, there was a diversity in their execution and interpretation. The AME Church, for example, splintered into two main sects along the line of African repatriation. The AME Zionist Church was emphatic about colonization in the United States and rejected "back to Africa."[8] The new sect chose to philosophically repatriate in ritual and memory. Black migration and colonization that extended into the US–Mexico Borderland regions brought with it Afrotopic notions of sovereignty.

Many mythologized narratives project the story of Moses in the book of Exodus. This study assumes Black folk went further into their biblical teachings and drew significance from the book of Joshua, as well. Guided in religious fervor, Black men enlisted as soldiers in an occupation force on Indigenous desert lands. Entrance into frontier spaces required an internal narrative of what to do after Moses died. Significant in the development of Afro-Frontiers, chaplains (Black ministers who were also military personnel) accompanied Black military personnel. Part of US expansionism in the 1870s, Black men served in all-Black military units and were empowered by the experience. Participation in confiscation and occupation of Indigenous lands redirected Black migration and colonization westward.

The common frameworks shaping the historiography of Black people in frontier spaces are rooted in a desire to document the existence of Black people who migrated to frontier spaces—leaving much to be desired, however, in the form of analysis. The idea that Black migration out of the South was an exodus was first publicly mentioned in the *Proceedings of the Select Committee of the United States Senate to Investigate the Causes of the Removal of the Negroes from the Southern States to the Northern States* in 1880.[9] Later, Black scholars such as Carter G. Woodson adapted the use of "Exodus" as a characterization of Black migration that took place in the fifty-year period surrounding

1900. His book, *A Century of Negro Migration*, was one of the earliest scholarly works to specifically cover the topic of mass Black migration.[10] In addition, he popularized the notion of Exodus as early as 1918. Woodson began his book with a chapter on Black people titled "Finding a Place of Refuge," and he ended it with a chapter on "The Exodus during the World War," referring to World War I.

BLACK MILITARY IN MEXICO'S NORTHER FRONTIER

Black military personnel, ministers, and Freemasons, through military service, transported themselves into the US westward expansion during America's postbellum period. On July 28, 1866, Black military personnel who served in the Union Army successfully lobbied the US Congress to authorize organization of Black regiments.[11] In 1869, Buffalo Soldier regiments of the 24th and 25th Infantry began the wave of mostly Black men in military service after the demise of major slave institutions. White officers lorded over the Black enlistees until the late 1870s when Henry O. Flipper commissioned as an officer from West Point and ushered in a new age of Black officers in the US military.

Texas was a kinetic frontier space where Black colonization was a part of the condition of Blackness. Freedom colonies in the state numbered in the hundreds by 1900. In part due to White violence, often military personnel led a colonization effort as if establishing a fort or fiefdom. Black military units were accompanied by military chaplains, many of whom were Freemasons. Black Freemasonry was a fundamental element to colonization efforts as the institution helped solidify the community's moral compass outside of church.

Significant to the frontier thesis, in 1784, in Boston, Massachusetts, Prince Hall Freemasonry was established on the Black side of town, parallel to White Freemasons, with full rights and authority to do so. Black frontier success bred envy in White Freemasons who also were White supremacists and a part of the second wave of the Ku Klux Klan at the turn of the twentieth century. The two fraternal orders retained similar names, as well as rituals and regalia independent of one another. When the newly established higher order was created in the late 1800s, White men attempted to restrict Black 32nd degree Freemasons from the Scottish Rite consistory or Knights Templar. White Freemasons argued they held legal and exclusive rights.

During America's racial nadir, White people did not stop at lynching, rape, and torture; they also attacked Black institutions with a similar violence. Such was the case when Black Freemasons adopted a higher order of 33rd Degree Freemasonry: The Ancient Egyptian Arabic Order of Nobles of the Mystic Shrine (Shriners). White Freemasons organized their charitable organization during the early 1870s in New York led by their Imperial Council. Black Freemasons in Chicago established a similar order that spread across the United States and maintained an Imperial Council with added authority from an ancient order of Mohammedans (Moors/Black Muslims) dating back to the seventh century.

At the turn of the twentieth century, White Freemasons attempted to strip Black Freemasons from using the names and regalia they both shared. White Freemasons filed a lawsuit that went to the US Supreme Court and was decided in 1929.[12] Both groups had local, grand, and supreme lodges "including Knights Templar and Scottish Rite consistories." In 1893, Black Freemasons incorporated their organization in Illinois successfully. In 1895, for White Freemasons who attempted to incorporate in New York, "the proffered incorporation was rejected." In 1901, Black Freemasons incorporated as a fraternal and charitable association under the May 5, 1870, Act of Congress. Court proceedings revealed that the Imperial Potentate of the White Shriners mentioned Black Shriners in national meetings, and nothing was done to show they had exclusive rights.

Black military personnel served in the Spanish–American War that began in 1898 and had a significant presence when the United States entered World War I on April 6, 1917. Some Black soldiers stayed overseas after the war and built colonies where they settled in Europe.

Military service did little to deter the ravages of White supremacy in the United States, however. Deadly as the flu pandemic was raging at the time, White violence against Black soldiers was swift. Sometimes Black military personnel were lynched in their uniforms on their way back from war. On December 11, 1917, Corporal Charles Baltimore was murdered by the local authorities in Texas. Houston police fatally wounded Corporal Baltimore—a member of the 24th US Infantry Regiment of Buffalo Soldiers—who had been defending a Black woman from police violence. Black military men began a protest in the city, which devolved into a deadly conflict. After most of the Black military men were court-martialed, thirteen were secretly hanged at dawn for treason. The 24th Infantry was then restricted from serving overseas.

Military service was the major vehicle to transport Black colonizers into an Afro-Frontier space.

> Reported out of Huntingdon, Pennsylvania on Tuesday, April 10, 1928, "U.S. Negro Colony Growing in Paris"
> Paris, April. —The American negro colony in Paris is growing by leaps and bounds. The World War began it. Many of the negroes came over to Oghi and Paris, liked them and either decided to stay over, or went back home and then returned. There is no distinction of color in the French capital. Life is pleasant and comparatively easy for them since jazz began its reign.
>
> The negro colony is naturally up in Montmartre where nearly all of the members work and ear[n] their daily bread. They are musicians and dancers, to a large extent, restaurant-keepers, doormen, and bootblacks. There are some cooks, tailors and a few students down near Boulevard St. Michel. Walking around the Place Pigalle at night one meets entire negro families. Sometimes they sit in their favorite cafes, sipping a beer or coffee, talking of the latest jazz hits and bootleggers back home.[13]

Wherever Black military personnel went, so too went Black Freemasonry as an omnipresent element of Black folks' collective "colonizer" consciousness.

White Freemasons in Arkansas filed a lawsuit in 1914 while Black Freemasons continued their growth; the suit was filed in part because Black Freemasonry had grown large enough that it made the White Shriners' argument of exclusive rights less believable. Size mattered in a system that recognized the leviathan. Ultimately, the final decree of the court stripped away all rights of Black Shriners to continue in name or full regalia in 1929. The adverse ruling did little to deter Black Freemasonry, which continues to the present day. The fraternity's secrecy, however, has led to an oversight in the recognition of its importance in the development of Black communities and in frontier spaces.

In January 1918, White Freemasons in Houston filed a similar lawsuit to restrict Black Freemasons from the higher order. Black Freemasons argued the White order never received exclusive rights, explicit in the order's Texas incorporation in 1902. This time, Texas state courts recognized the rights of Black Freemasons. The court opinion recognized the two orders were similar, but it did not see a violation of state law. Nevertheless, courts found White Freemasons did have a superior and exclusive right to their version. Most notably, the Supreme Court case forced Black Freemasons to reveal their membership and wealth. The corporate veil of the fraternity allowed Black Freemasons of the 33rd Degree to grow to 9,000 members who were all exposed to targeted acts. The corporate veil allowed Black Freemasons to build a real estate empire that included seventy-six lodges valued at about $600,000 ($10,000,000 today).

> Negro "Shriners" Are Enjoined | Houston, Tex., March 25, 1922.
> By the Associated Press:
> HOUSTON, Tex., March 25—A temporary injunction restraining negro Shriners, so called, from wearing the Shrine Emblem and

> from using organization names peculiar to the Shrine was granted Saturday by Judge Ewing Boyd in District Court.[14]

The condition of American Blackness assumed second-class citizenship in the United States. However, in the US–Mexico Borderlands, citizenship of any class was still citizenship. Unlike White spaces that produced a Black/White binary, the Borderlands produced a citizenship privilege in relationship with that of the noncitizen. In frontier spaces of the Spanish-speaking Borderlands, Whiteness was not the singular source of hegemonic power. American Blackness grew increasingly powerful as the US military ranks exploded with Black people in service to their government. In coordination with colonization efforts, Black people had little doubt in their ability for self-governance. Black institutions nurtured Afro-notions of God's promise. Contextualized by US westward expansion, Ethiopianism had a new frontier space to inspire Afrotopia.[15]

AFROTOPIA AND DUALITY IN MEXICO'S NORTHERN FRONTIER

Karl Jacoby, in his book *The Strange Career of William Ellis: The Texas Slave Who Became a Mexican Millionaire*, recognized the life of a wealthy Black man at the turn of the twentieth century. William Ellis was born June 15, 1864, on the plantation of Charles and Margaret Nelson Ellis, under the institution of slavery in Victoria, Texas. He worked alongside Tejano ranchers growing up, learning Spanish and also becoming known as Guillermo Eliseo.

William/Guillermo attended college and studied business in Nashville, Tennessee, as well as in New York. In 1888, William/Guillermo grew his ranching empire and network from Texas to New Mexico to Arizona before expanding further south into Mexico's northern frontier. In 1890, William/Guillermo held a meeting with President Porfirio Díaz to persuade him to allow Black colonization in Mexico's north.[16]

William/Guillermo died a Gilded Age Manhattanite, wealthy from a few mining operations in Mexico. He was known to live in a penthouse apartment overlooking New York's Central Park. He was part of a cohort of ambitious Black people who used institutions to veil their personal striving from their conditions of Blackness.

William/Guillermo's career was neither strange nor unique, as he used the US border to shield his Afrotopic strivings in Mexico. His trajectory intersected with various racialization projects taking place in the US–Mexico Borderlands. He embodied the transformation of Mexico's northern frontier into the US territory as it continued to persist as a Spanish-speaking borderland. As a border-dweller, he found privilege and opportunity with his use of language. Fluent in Spanish, in 1895 he spearheaded a colonization scheme 600 miles south of Chaves County, New Mexico, in Tlahualilo, Durango, Mexico under the leadership of Texas AME Church Bishop Henry Turner. He recruited nearly 1,000 Black folks who were mostly from Alabama. William/Guillermo's recruitment pipeline of people came from well-known emigration agent R. A. "Pegleg" Williams. William/Guillermo and the Black migrants who followed him to Tlahualilo subscribed to Ethiopianist notions.

William/Guillermo internalized liberation theology and led the colonization effort. After a false start at colonizing Mexico's northern frontier around 1890, due in part to a lack of support and of funding, William/Guillermo finally achieved Afrotopia with a colony in Tlahualilo, Durango, Mexico. However, little was achieved before Mexican militias seized power over the colony. Dystopia and chaos were reported back to the United States on May 3, 1895, in the *Taylor County News* (Abilene, Texas); the headline read, "Poor Deluded Negroes":

> A negro boy who escaped from the negro colony in Mexico (mention of which was made in these columns when the negroes were moving hence) gives a startling account of the deplorable condition of the poor negroes who were tricked into the enterprise. The boy's account given in an interview with the *Houston Post*, is in effect:

> that the negroes are poorly fed, poorly clothed, camped in herds, without shelter, worked from daylight until dark, and all the time under strict guard by Mexicans, armed. The poor negroes did not know what real slavery was until they reached Mexico as so-called colonists. The United States Government should take immediate steps to ascertain if the assertions of this boy are true—and then see to it that the negroes have justice and that speedily.[17]

After the disaster of his first colonization attempts, William/Guillermo traveled to Ethiopia in search of a new frontier space to exploit and build wealth once more. While there in 1903, William/Guillermo met with King Menlik II and negotiated business deals in the textile industry. His work led to cotton-growing and an ambassadorship.

William/Guillermo also negotiated a repatriation effort for Black people to Africa and specifically Ethiopia, which epitomized African utopia throughout the nineteenth-century continuum of Black colonization events. William/Guillermo brokered a deal with the United States government to carry out the scheme and augment relations between the two countries. His diplomatic work and ambitions bought him a seat on the New York Stock Exchange for $45,000 or (about $2,000,000 today).

Black colonization efforts ballooned into projects across the planet. In 1895, at the same time that William Ellis advertised his colonization efforts, Matthew Lancaster pitched an "American Negro Colony" in Brazil:

> St. Louis, June 12—Matthew Lancaster, an intelligent and well-educated negro, has been quietly corresponding for some months with persons controlling large tracts of land in Brazil, and has announced his purpose of colonizing American negroes upon these lands. Mr. Lancaster leaves for Brazil next Monday, armed with strong testimonials and financial backing. The project is favorably received by the negroes here.[18]

Matthew's life might appear as "strange" as William/Guillermo's; however, through the lens of Afro-Frontierism, the two of them represent a large cohort of Black colonizers who were scattered across the planet seeking Afrotopia. When Black communities nurture institutions in agreement with Black ministers, military personnel, and Black Freemasons, autonomy projects abound.

On June 22, 1897, the *Denver Republican* reported on "A Negro Colony for Wyoming."[19] Agent Bryan represented the group who had come from the South and had arrived in Laramie. They sought to purchase 25,000 acres of land and live out their Afrotopic dreams. Autonomy projects were a key part of all Black enclaves including those situated in the American South. The *Atlanta Constitution* reported on November 7, 1897, "Negro Colony in Alabama."[20] The colony was funded by Mrs. Lillian K. Ray, "the wealthy English lady who represents a syndicate of English capitalists." The colony of Cedar Lake had a formal opening with a city charter and a provisional board of directors. On 800 acres a few hundred Black folks lived out their version of Afrotopia.

CHAPTER 2

PRECONDITIONS

On October 16, 1903, the *Hereford Reporter* noted, "New Mexico to Have Nigger Town": "The Blackdom Townsite Company with F. M. Bayer [*sic*, Boyer], A. M. President proposes to establish a town exclusively for negroes in Chaves County, near the line of the Pecos Valley railroad. The opening will occur May 1, 1904, at which time the promoters propose to locate 10,000 negroes."[1]

BLACKDOM ONTOLOGY AND THE NIAGARA MOVEMENT (1905–1909)

In the early 1900s, Black activists/intellectuals envisioned greater progress for people under the conditions of American Blackness. Wealthy White elites often funded and encouraged mutual aid projects that made a few Black folks wealthy in the process. Most notably, Booker T. Washington and his leadership at the Tuskegee Institute found fame and fortune as wealthy White elites helped him promote Black progress—through labor, for the most part.

Other less well-funded Black intellectuals devised alternative articulations to problematize Washington's perceived limited view. In 1905, out of an intellectual activism grew the Niagara Movement, led by activist scholars such as Mary Burnett Talbert, William Monroe Trotter, Gertrude Morgan, and W. E. B. Du Bois. As a group, they organized an intellectual defense for the value of the ontology of Black folks. Grappling with the trappings of integration and the burdens of segregation, the Niagara Movement grew to over 170 members in thirty-four states of the Union.[2] Part of the mystique of the short-lived movement was in the name that captured the struggle. In the US northern borderland, unable to book a meeting in Buffalo, New York, the group crossed into Canada. In America's northern borderland, the Niagara Movement developed to shape notions of an intellectual Blackness. Many of the movement's leaders, including W.E.B. Du Bois, would later apply their Niagara Movement experience to helping create the National Association for the Advancement of Colored People (NAACP).[3]

NEW MEXICO BORDERLANDS AND THE BIRTH OF BLACKDOM

At the turn of the twentieth century, Black folks' excogitation of a Black domain in frontier space evolved from an adequate set of circumstances to produce Afrotopia in Chaves County. Blackdomites believed that God, citizen conditions, collective knowledge, land, and labor were enough to start their autonomy project. New Mexico was a US territory and local jurisdictions were restricted from full enforcement of Jim Crow laws. Also, while the Black population was minuscule, their occupation of Indigenous lands was useful to colonization efforts in the Borderlands. Black folks understood the American Blackness condition in the territory was enhanced by self-segregation. The Blackdom Townsite Company was part of the scheme to harness Black power at the intersection of Black ministers, Black military personnel, and Black Freemasons. Moreover, incorporation helped erect a corporate virtual veil—separating Blackdomites from the unique conditions of American Blackness in New Mexico—to participate unencumbered in generational wealth creation during boom times.

Blackdomites expected to take full advantage of citizenship without the impositions of a "White-dominated" society. Black folks became landlords and matured their investment while exploiting the race/citizenship loophole in the territory. The Blackdom Townsite Company was a physical manifestation of their most noble Afrocentric ideals. In 1903, Frank Boyer was intimately familiar with colonization of Mexico's northern frontier when he became one of thirteen Blackdom co-founders. Frank had trained as a minister/soldier and brought with him Prince Hall Freemasonry. Stories about Frank Boyer and his relationship to Blackdom often offer to audiences myths of both. Instead, this narrative begins during the Civil War, before Frank was born, when the Boyer family was enslaved on the Elias Boyer plantation in Georgia. In this chapter we explore the infancy of Blackdomites' Afro-Frontier to further reconcile the relationship between Black towns and prophets.

Confederates established themselves in the West, particularly in Oklahoma, Texas, and Arizona. Homesteading allowed tens of thousands to become first-time landowners in New Mexico as well. Lack of water access, however, made desert land hard to prove up and led to only a small land occupation compared to their claims of Manifest Destiny. Black people found opportunity as federal authorities loosened restrictions to land "ownership." As frontier sovereigns and landlords in the US–Mexico Borderlands, Black people transitioned from colonized people to colonizers. The chaos of westward expansion and discombobulation of Native and Indigenous communities tremendously benefited Black folks even as second-class citizens.

The southeastern section of the New Mexico Territory was sparsely populated due in part to lack of access to water. Genocidal military campaigns against the Mescalero Apaches had resolved into a reservation condition as newly drawn county borders began to reinforce their incarceration. In 1877, as American Reconstruction came to a close, Confederate Army Captain Joseph Lea moved to the village of Roswell, in Lincoln County. Captain Lea was one of the earliest influencers in the development of Chaves County (part of what was Lincoln County). By 1885, he helped the village transition Roswell into a platted city.

The region had been in chaos after the trials of the Lincoln County War. Myths developed within the framework of the "Lincoln County Wars" are beyond the scope of this study. However, "Lincoln County" was a regional phenomenon that shaped the course of New Mexico's history during the late nineteenth century. Essentially, "White" colonizers converged on stolen Indigenous land. Most notably, the trial of Billy the Kid occupied the imagination of the era's end. Significant to this study, Southern New Mexico developed into a Confederate sympathizer–inspired stable space to build a Southern-styled oasis.

Captain Lea helped bring stability and Confederate sentiments to Roswell. He co-founded the Goss Military Institute (now the New Mexico Military Institute), named for Confederate Colonel Robert Goss. In 1895, James J. Hagerman, a tycoon who made a fortune in Colorado, bought forty acres in Roswell, and donated the land to grow the size of the campus. James Hagerman's investment in the New Mexico Military Institute (NMMI) ensured federal investment in the region as part of a network of military outposts in Mexico's northern frontier.

After 1890, James Hagerman became a chief investor in Charles B. Eddy Pecos Irrigation and Investment Company to further help develop the region. In the newly created Pecos Irrigation and Improvement Company, James Hagerman negotiated the largest irrigation project in the United States at the time. Hagerman led the efforts to engineer a sustainable water supply for two irrigation systems. The first was a forty-mile long, thirty-five feet wide system that carried seven feet of water. The second was forty-five miles south of the first irrigation project and was forty miles long and forty-five feet wide at the bottom, and also carried seven feet of water. The Pecos River fed both projects and flowed at 1,000 cubic feet per second. Three reservoirs supplying the intervening space were under construction. The massive undertaking by Hagerman required an investment of more than a million dollars (about $26,000,000 today). The United States congressional report on this project ended with the prospect that, "No one can even imagine what New Mexico will produce when her immense acreage of fertile soil is brought under cultivation through enterprises of this kind."[24]

Stability encouraged the emigration of tycoons such as John Chisum, a cattle rancher who dominated the market at the time. Chisum lobbied for specific railroad paths and station locations advantageous to his empire in the last quarter of the 1800s. When railways were established in the Pecos Valley Region, Chisum's fortune grew exponentially. Railroads opened new desert frontier spaces for occupation and propelled migration to Southeastern New Mexico.

James Hagerman, who moved to Chaves County in 1892, bought and expanded Chisum's Roswell ranch and changed the name to Old South Springs Ranch. Hagerman expanded his fortune with investment in the region after finishing Hagerman Pass, a railroad penetrating the Rocky Mountains from Colorado Springs. Hagerman sold his shares of Colorado Midland Railway to the Atchison, Topeka, and Santa Fe Railway and began the Pecos Valley Railroad that was completed in 1894. Hagerman pooled investments from the Pullman Car Company and a group of investors led by Benjamin Cheney of American Express. For $250,000 (about $7,000,000 today) in bonds, Hagerman paid the Santa Fe Railroad Company for construction material.

The Santa Fe Railroad Company controlled a 370-mile-long feeder from Amarillo to Pecos and connected with the company's Southern Kansas Line. The Pecos Valley Railway and its extension allowed the company to control shipping routes in the New Mexico cattle industry. By 1899, with a 200-mile extension of the Northeastern Railway from Roswell to Amarillo, Roswell sustained a direct connection with Denver, Kansas City, St Louis, and Chicago. Wherever the railroad stopped, populations grew out of necessity and began with machine shops, roundhouses, and railroad offices. Roswell had now developed into a central point of the region's economic infrastructure, fundamental to the supply chain of the Pecos Valley Region. Moreover, Chaves

County became the conduit for community growth from mass migration by train.

A diversity of companies, from the Tallmadge Immigration Company to the Aztec Cattle Company, established offices in Roswell as it became the most economically dominant place in all of New Mexico at the time. By 1900, Chaves County exported close to a million pounds of wool per year. The region was also abundant in farms harvesting alfalfa, fruits, and vegetables. Even more lucrative was the city's position linking silver and gold mines as well as coalfields with the junction of the El Paso and Northeastern Railway. Water was a challenge for communities outside the range of the water network for the Pecos River that flowed southeasterly through the region. James Hagerman's investment in water irrigation projects was the undercurrent responsible for the explosion of land occupation and sustained migration.[5]

The Hagerman family wealth grew along with their political influence. James's son Herbert graduated from Cornell University in 1890 and moved to the Hagerman ranch in Chaves County. From 1898 to 1901, Herbert was the secretary at the US Embassy to Russia where Nikolai II Alexandrovich Romanov (Czar Nicholas II) presented him with the coveted Russian Order of Saint Anna. In 1906, James and Herbert used their influence to get Herbert appointed as seventeenth governor of New Mexico Territory, which guaranteed growth in southeastern New Mexico.[6] Frank Boyer had returned to the Borderlands and took a job as a cook in the Hagerman household sometime between 1900 and 1903.

Chaves County was in the midst of boom times, and ambitious people went there in hopes of growing their wealth. Roswell's wealthy families were as cosmopolitan and consumer driven as people in major cities. Often, they were transplants from the cities, coming west in search of new opportunities and/or to preserve old fortunes. Elite Roswellians bought luxury items from England, France, and various parts of Asia. Some Roswellians were among the first in the country to use electricity, have the latest in technological advancements, and travel paved roads. In 1901, Dr. W. E. Parkhurst from Lansing, Michigan, was the first person to pull up in a car: an Oldsmobile.

Racial strife in Texas pushed a few groups of Black migrants into the New Mexico Territory in the late nineteenth century. The motivation for the migration to Eastern New Mexico was mostly proximity and a keen sense of opportunity specific to citizenship laws and borders in the Pecos Valley Region. For example, cattle baron John Chisum moved his family to Roswell to raise children with his wife Jensie, who was Black. This Chisum family started with John as an inheritor of slaves. John Chisum exploited New Mexico's lack of Jim Crow laws to occupy space between New Mexican racism and the law of the land to raise a family in sovereignty.

Frank Chisum, John's son, was a part of early Blackdomite colonization efforts as witness on Isaac Jones' homestead proving-up papers.[7] Although Chaves County was an ex-Confederate stronghold, New Mexicanity and federal law made it difficult for White supremacy to flourish in the territory unimpeded. Southern culture that produced the vilest and most depraved atrocities against Black bodies was rare in Eastern New Mexico during America's racial nadir. Black people had the authority to pursue their striving in ways other parts of the United States could not accommodate.

New Mexico's total population, as recorded from the census of 1900 to the census of 1910, increased 68 percent (195,310 to 327,301). During the same time, the Black population rose from 1,610 to 1,628. Even though the Black population seemed to have plateaued in growth, there was a demographic shift from rural to urban areas. In 1890, Black people in urban areas totaled 274. In 1900, the Black population in urban areas increased to 581, and by 1910, the population had increased to 795. Between 1900 and 1910, Chaves County's population went from 4,773 to 16,850. The Black population of Chaves County in 1900 was 66 and grew to 233 by 1910 (52 mulattos and 181 negroes). By 1910, the male to female ratio was almost even, 125 males and 108 females. After 1900, growth in the county allowed for sustainable family units.

CHAPTER 2

BLACKDOM HISTORY AND FRANK BOYER

Popular myths and stories about Frank Boyer project a mishmash of tropes wrapped in competing agendas. The Boyer/Blackdom myths borrow from the Exoduster paradigm to reconstruct the narrative trajectory of a hero's journey.[8] Written through the lens of Exodusterism, chronicles have prioritized the role of Moses-like figures and incorporated small parts of Frank's real life. Blackdom's common narratives start with Frank, in a trajectory to suggest that New Mexico was the gateway to his "promised land," Blackdom. The Old South functioned as the backdrop and motivating force to push him westward.

Mythologizing Frank Boyer has value beyond the scope of this study. A newly discovered interview with Frank Boyer in 1947 guides this Afro-Frontier narrative to separate Frank's life and Blackdom's full trajectory. Functioning as a first draft of history, Frank's last interview strung together key points in his life, including Blackdom Townsite Company and Blackdom Oil Company (newly discovered). Stories about Blackdom have a wide range of start dates. How the author understood Frank Boyer's story often dictated most of their speculations. For this study, Blackdom, New Mexico, was an all-Black frontier town that began in 1903, on September 5, with the incorporation of the Blackdom Townsite Company.

In 1986, Daniel Gibson wrote "Blackdom," an essay that began the story of Blackdom in 1896. Supposedly, Frank Boyer was forced to flee his home state of Georgia. According to Gibson, Frank's involuntary migration began as the Ku Klux Klan (KKK) threatened his life. With brother-in-law Daniel Keys, husband to Francis M. Boyer's (Frank Boyer's) sister, the two men journeyed out of the South. Gibson's narrative concoctions indulge in the myth for a few reasons. Most significantly, in the New Mexico statehood grand narrative, the Boyer/Blackdom myth helps project "the Land of Enchantment" marketing scheme. According to Frank in 1947, he was "proud of the fact that relationship between the White and Negro residents of that section of Georgia always has been good. There has never been a lynching within the borders of the county."[9] The myth of Boyer's KKK encounter began a narrative trajectory that had little to do with Frank's story and by extension Blackdom's history. Convenient in the Boyer/Blackdom myth was also an appearance of fecklessness and failure when Boyer left Chaves County in the second decade of the experiment.

By 2000, a survey of early stories about Blackdom collectively described an epic heroes' journey, on the part of Boyer and a few others. Problematically, scholars began to echo the Boyer/Blackdom myth that grew to include a 2,000-plus-mile walk from Pelham, Georgia, to Roswell, New Mexico. Boyer's motivation to build Blackdom was implied as a byproduct of Frank's need for refuge from White supremacy. The conflation of the Boyer/Blackdom myth lends itself to telling a story that ends in the early 1920s. Around 1922, Frank left Chaves County to build in Vado, New Mexico (Doña Ana County). Many authors assumed his departure was in the wake of Blackdom's collapse. My research suggests that Frank left the Afro-Frontier town in the hands of the next generation of Boyers, and a host of new Black folks who stayed in Chaves County and entered the homestead class.

A History of Blackdom, N.M. in the Context of the African American Post Civil War Colonization Movement was published by the Historic Preservation Division of the Office of Cultural Affairs in Santa Fe, as the State of New Mexico commissioned histories for an upcoming centennial celebration of statehood in 2012.[10] Maisha Baton and Native American historian Henry J. Walt dominated the footnotes of Blackdom's historiography. Purportedly, droughts were the impetus of Frank's departure and the decline of Blackdom. Early stories about Blackdom end with Frank in Vado around 1922. Boyer/Blackdom stories superimpose the real drought conditions after 1916 in Chaves County to push Frank's migration once more. His departure marked Blackdom's decline and defined the final chapter. The Boyer/Blackdom narrative perpetuates a simple telling of both stories and was written to serve a narrow agenda of promoting New Mexico as modern while keeping intact the tricultural approach.

The Boyer/Blackdom narrative fit into the account New Mexico wanted to tell. In December 1996, the Public Broadcasting Service (PBS) in New Mexico sponsored a documentary for the ¡Colores! segment to tell the story of Blackdom.[11] Billed as the chronicle of Frank and Ella Boyer's dream, it plotted the moments of the all-Black town in relationship with Boyer's fictitious life. The tagline attributed to Frank: "There was no one to help us and no one to hinder." In February 2013 (Black History Month), *Smithsonian* magazine (online) echoed the Boyer/Blackdom myth. Following a series of Boyer/Blackdom retellings, Frank's mythology produced ascribed quotes such as, "Here the black man has an equal chance with the White man. Here you are reckoned at the value which you place upon yourself. Your future is in your own hands." Whether these were Frank's words or not, the sentiment was useful in marketing New Mexico as a somewhat inclusive brand.

FRANK

Anchored in the written record of Frank Boyer's life, his story begins with Aggie Boyer (Frank's grandmother), who was born sovereign in Africa and forced into the trans-Atlantic slave trade. In Milledgeville, Georgia, Aggie begot Henry Boyer (Frank's father). The youngest of seventeen children, Frank was the firstborn free. At the age of 77, Frank sat in 1947 with Kathryn Henry, a reporter for the *Clovis News-Journal*. Frank's interview appeared in that periodical and was reprinted in the Doña Ana County newspaper of record, *Las Cruces Sun-News*.[12] Frank bragged about his grandchildren, who numbered one for every year Frank spent on Earth. Through his refinement of formal knowledge as a minister, soldier, and Freemason, Frank became a colonizer. In his fifty years in the Borderlands, Frank helped plat Fort Huachuca in his youth, Blackdom in his prime years, and the city of Clovis during his later years.

Archetypical of Black colonizers, Frank Boyer had prior military service before helping to build Blackdom. Frank boasted about his time rounding up "Indian insurrectionists" of the "famous 'Crazy

Snake Rebellion' in the Creek Nation of Indian Territory," currently Henryetta, Oklahoma. Frank left the Borderlands and returned to Georgia where he attended Atlanta Baptist College, now Morehouse College—a historically black college/university (HBCU)—sponsored by Superior Court Judge Logan Bleckley. During college, Frank worked as a proofreader at the old *Atlanta Constitution*. Ella McGruder, three years younger than Frank, graduated from the Haines Institute. The couple married and began a family in Georgia. Frank's pre-Blackdom period was formulaic in how Black colonizers emerged from Black communities with White people in their periphery. Frank was a product of intersectional Blackness.

Some myths were created by happenstance. Kathryn Henry of the *Clovis News-Journal* interviewed Frank in Vado, New Mexico, two years before his passing. According to Frank, he and Daniel Keys traveled back to New Mexico together. Kathryn wrote, "[Frank] and a companion [Daniel Keys] walked from Southwestern Georgia to Abilene, Texas, a distance of 2,178 miles." Kathryn was of a younger generation and may have misunderstood Frank's explanation of his trek from Georgia. Her next sentence read, "They 'beat the freights' from Abilene, Texas, and then walked from Pecos to Eddy [County], now Carlsbad in the New Mexico Territory." The phrase "beat the freights" identified the cheap way in Frank's day to travel by train. Perhaps the story reflected the sentiment of traveling from Georgia to the Pecos Valley Region, but Frank had more means, motive, and manner than to walk the whole 2,000-plus-mile distance.

Among Frank Boyer's first jobs were as cook for James Hagerman and buggy driver for US District Judge Alfred Freeman. Frank was thus consciously in the presence of power brokers. Judge Freeman held court in Lincoln and Socorro Counties as well as Las Cruces. In 1877, Judge Freeman was the US consul in Prague, Bohemia. He was also appointed assistant US attorney general. After the US Congress created a new associate justice position for New Mexico, President Benjamin Harrison appointed Judge Freeman to the bench in October 1890 where he served a four-year term. Judge Freeman and his son-in-law, James Cameron, started a law practice in Eddy County (Carlsbad after 1899). Judge Freeman and Frank Boyer traveled by buggy and camped in the mountains when night overtook them en route from one place to another. Freeman's long career afforded Boyer some access to knowledge in how to effectively colonize the Borderlands through corporatocracy and navigation through bureaucracy.

Judge Freeman had become one of the most powerful men in New Mexico when he became a fixture in Chaves County. The sixteenth governor of New Mexico Territory, Miguel Antonio Otero, chose Judge Freeman to lobby in Washington, DC, against the building of a dam on the Rio Grande River. In 1904, a group of lawyers in Chaves County sponsored Judge Freeman's nomination to the position of associate justice in the newly created congressionally mandated judicial district headquartered in Roswell. Frank's work for Judge Freeman was a side hustle as he began his journey towards sovereignty.

In September 1903, Blackdomites incorporated the Blackdom Townsite Company, and a month later, the *Santa Fe New Mexican* reported, "The Son of Judge Freeman Sends a Bullet Through His Heart at His Home in Carlsbad." Hugh Freeman—Judge Freeman's son—was thirty years of age. A few years after the tragedy, the Freeman family moved away from New Mexico. As Frank neared the end of his first homestead process, in 1907, Judge Freeman retired to British Columbia where he had invested in the lumber industry. When Judge Freeman withdrew from the New Mexico bar in early 1908, Frank completed his final homestead proving-up papers.

In Blackdom's infancy, Frank Boyer employed the power of position as president of "the Only Exclusive Negro Settlement in New Mexico." Frank maintained a handpump surface well that provided a sufficient amount of water for the land he rented while working for the Hagerman enterprise and Judge Freeman. However, the opportunity of Blackdom required Frank to homestead and not simply rent land. Inability to reach a significant water source separated him from Afrotopia on his homestead land. The land was at a higher elevation than the canal built to sustain the farms in the area.

Behind the corporate veil of Blackdom Townsite Company, Frank procured a more powerful pump to go deeper and access water needed to grow a surplus of crops. In 1904, he wrote to Leary, Gill, and Marrow in Roswell, a water pump supplier, from his position as president of the only exclusive Negro settlement in the US territory of New Mexico.[13] Frank's letter helped him leverage the idea of Blackdom and the town's expected May 1904 opening to procure an engine for a more powerful well pump. His hand pump went twelve feet deep and needed to go twenty-five feet deep. Frank Boyer did not have the money for the "Jack of all trades" pump, quoted at a price of $160. In the letter, Frank asserted, "You have the engine, I have the water, farm, and skill and labor." Frank was conscious of his new credibility underwritten by the newly created position of President in the Blackdom Townsite Company. As a successful farmer and businessman, Frank raised $12,000 to help establish the Afro-Frontier town of Blackdom.

"NEW MEXICO TO HAVE NIGGER TOWN"

Weaving the lives of Blackdomites together presents a mosaic that helps to interpret common activities. Frank Boyer's emphatic use of the phrase "the only exclusive Negro settlement in New Mexico" affirms an Afrocentricity in the Blackdomite movement. On September 5, 1903, Francis M. Boyer, Isaac W. Jones, Daniel G. Keys, Burrel Dickerson, Charles C. Childress, John A. Boyer, James Jackson, Charles W. Clifton, Charles Thompson, Albert Hubert, Benjamin Harrison, George White, and Joseph Cook were signers to the Blackdom Townsite Company's Articles of Incorporation. They bought stock as part of their membership in the company.

Blackdomites bought into a common cause and were expected to help plat a town square "with additions into blocks, lots, streets, alleys, avenues, commons, parks, and public grounds and to own, hold, sell, and convey said lots and blocks and improve the same." Blackdomites sought to "purchase, sell, improve, cultivate and colonize lands" to underwrite their economy. Blackdomites planned for vast irrigation projects to take advantage of the system of artesian wells along with the construction of reservoirs, canals, and ditches for the sale of water rights. Blackdomites also saved space for education through the college level "to improve the health, welfare, and prosperity of such inhabitants."[14] Blackdom was an organized business to meet the needs of a Black colonizer community.

After the incorporation of the Blackdom Townsite Company, Blackdomites publicized advertisements that traveled from the State of Washington to South Carolina. By September 11, 1903, a few days after incorporation, all of Indiana was flooded with advertisements promoting the Afro-Frontier town. In July 1903, Evansville had descended into war drawn along racial lines. White violence exploded as the recently settled Black migrants continued to build their community. Whitelash resulted in the death of both Black and White people as Black folks fought violence with violence. While Blackdomites blanketed all of Indiana with a sea of advertisements, Isaac Jones began the first homestead connected to Blackdom.

To clarify a significant detail about Blackdom's early years, according to homestead final proofing documents, none of the early homesteaders connected their land to the municipality called Blackdom. For example, Isaac Jones completed his homestead patent in 1905. Under threat of federal perjury charges and possibly land fraud, on question 8 of his testimony to the land office in Chaves County ("Is your present claim within the limits of an incorporated town or selected site of a city or town or used in any way for trade and business?"), Isaac responded, "No, Sir."[15] The inconsistencies in Blackdom's early years (loosely referred to as the lost years) are complicated as more Blackdomites completed homestead patents that, technically, had nothing to do with Blackdom.

For Frank Boyer, who first rented land before proving up, the transition to homesteader was much smoother than that of Isaac Jones, who had to move his young family from Roswell to participate in the Blackdom colonization scheme. A Blackdomites' advertisement echoed an announcement from New Mexico's Office of the Territorial Secretary on September 9, 1903:

> The following articles of incorporation have been filed in the office of the Territorial secretary: The Blackdom Townsite company with a capital stock of $10,000 which is divided into 50,000 [5,000] shares of $2 each. The incorporators and directors are Francis M. Boyer, Isaac. W. Jones, Daniel G. Keys, Burrel Dickerson, Charles C. Childress, John A. Boyer, Charles Thompson, James Jackson, Charles Clifton, Albert Hubert, George White, Benjamin Harrison, and Joseph Cook. The objects of the company are to establish and operate the town of Blackdom in Chaves County, and to conduct a negro colony in that section. The term of the incorporation is fifty years and the principal place of business will be in the town of Blackdom when it is established. For the present, the offices will be located in Roswell.

Behind the corporate veil of the Blackdom Townsite Company, people under the conditions of American Blackness were recognized as sovereigns in the New Mexico Territory. The territorial secretary's official announcement about Blackdom's organization printed in the *Santa Fe New Mexican* was a synopsis of the announcement standardized into words copied by local newspapers. Blackdomites had their interpretation of the colonization scheme. The advertisements were filtered through various hegemonic institutions before local newspaper offices interpreted the Afrotopic information into headlines. At the Logansport *Pharos-Tribune* in Indiana on September 10, 1903, the headline read, "Here's Youre [*sic*] Segregation, Mr Graves":

> Santa Fe., N.M., Sept. 10. —The Blackdom Townsite company was incorporated with a capital stock of $10,000. The purpose is

> to establish a colony of negroes from the southern states in Chavez [*sic*] County, the name of town to be Blackdom.

No information as to who Mr. Graves might have been or the name of the headline writer was obtained, despite many attempts to identify them. On the same day, September 10, 1903, the *Latrobe* (Pennsylvania) *Bulletin* headline read, "Colony for Negroes," followed by the Blackdom Townsite blurb. As compared to the Indiana headline, Black colonization appeared less contentious in Pennsylvania.

On September 11, 1903, the *Sterling* (Illinois) *Gazette* reprinted reports from Santa Fe of the exclusive "Negro Colony," while in Decatur, Indiana, Blackdom was referred to as a "Negro Colonization Scheme." In Elkhart, Indiana, the headline read, "Refuge for Negroes"; in Silver Lake, Indiana, "Blackdom, a Negro Refuge," a consistent headline reprinted in Washington (Indiana), Connersville, New Albany, Knox, Logansport, Middlebury, and Flora. The US Midwest region was inundated with news about Blackdom Townsite Company's inception, but no state was more saturated than Indiana. Blackdomites appear to have found opportunity in the aftermath of the Evansville riot as they promoted a sovereign space as an alternative. Blackdomites nurtured a Black consciousness at the intersection of American Blackness and the New Mexico Territory, a borderland influenced by ministers, military men, and Black Freemasons.

CHAPTER 3

PROPHETS, PROFITS, AND THE PROFFIT FAMILY

This chapter returns to the master work of Kenneth Hamilton's *Black Towns and Profit* to introduce a postscript: the Afro-Frontier extended beyond his construct of the trans-Appalachian West. Generally, Blackdom's history provides a postscript to the Hamiltonian time frame of 1877 to 1915. The town of Blackdom existed into the Roaring Twenties. Through the exploration of documented activities, a collective unique Black consciousness emerged. As a Borderland study, Blackdom's history and Blackdomite records suggests Afrotopia was inspired by a longer history of Black institutions that supported notions of Black sovereignty. Vividly, the townsite projected a conscious embrace of Booker T. Washington's emphasis on Black labor as well as W. E. B. Du Bois's ascribed significance of Black ontology. In this chapter we will also excavate Blackdom's homestead-class intersection behind the corporate veil of Blackdom Townsite Company to contextualize the mundanity of homesteading and incorporation that transformed a rustic bourgeoisie.

Blackdom's incorporation provided names to cross-reference Chaves County land records and gain access to learn more about the original townsite developers of the scheme. Developers homesteaded and promoters bought into the idea of Blackdom but may not have bought into the full scheme. Once cross-referenced with names on homestead records, Blackdom's place in the region frames the window to view Blackdom. Detailed homestead records reflected the intentional pattern Black homesteaders adopted over time and helped tell this new story of Blackness in the Borderlands.

Black people on record was a sign of Blackdomite duality and reality as sovereign Black folks. Many residents of Blackdom experienced the institution of slavery or were the first born after the major institutions of slavery dissipated. The twoness of being recognized in a society that suggested they were second-class citizens sparked a cultural consciousness amongst Black folks with faith in God. Blackdomites believed and said "yes" to a fully immersive society built on intellectual growth and spiritual well-being as well as public social mobility. Blackdom was a proof of concept for the idea of self-governance and self-determination among "New Negro": Black folks.

THE PROFFIT FAMILY

There was once a family named Proffit who migrated and became Blackdomites. The first in the family to complete a homestead, William D. Proffit, patented 158.65 acres in December 1910. Eleven years later, in January 1921, William completed a second noncontiguous eighty acres less than a mile south of his original homestead. How does one reconcile the popular framework of Blackdom's abandonment in the 1920s and William Proffit's long-term investment in the scheme? Documents leave little with which to bridge gaps in information. The framework of Afro-Frontierism helps to buttress the significance lost in the mundanity of documents.

Recognizing the uniformity of Blackdomite society in the Afro-Frontier framework, the Proffit family's whole set of activities illuminates "Blackdom." Family patriarch and ordained minister from Mississippi William Proffit led his family to Chaves County in 1907. William was born under the institution of slavery and at the age of 51 began his homestead patent process in 1908. His daughter, Luberta Proffit completed a 319.60-acre homestead in 1915, followed by his son David (320 acres) in 1918, and daughter-in-law, Belle Billue Proffit (320 acres) in 1919. The land occupation suggests the family's ownership ambitions were fueled by the eventual development of a Negro oil company. A few months after Belle Proffit was granted her land patent, the Blackdom Township officially announced the organization of the Blackdom Oil Company.

Added to William Proffit's eighty-acre patent, the family's total land ownership included over one-and-a-half square miles of land. When Blackdom was in its revival post-1911, William Proffit was a pastor at Blackdom Baptist Church. The Proffit family thrived in Blackdom's boom times during the Roaring Twenties. Throughout the 1920s, William also maintained a household in Roswell, New Mexico, twenty miles north of Blackdom.

On July 15, 1929, the *Roswell Daily Record* ran William Proffit's obituary:

> "William Proffit Dies"
> William David Proffit, aged seventy-two years, passed away at his home, 600 South Michigan Street, yesterday morning at 3 o'clock. Mr. Proffit came to Roswell about twenty years ago from Mississippi and has been a familiar figure about the city. He was ordained Minister many years ago and has been pastor of the Colored Baptist

> Church for many years. He is survived by three sons [although only two are mentioned], David Proffit of Roswell, Isaac Mathew Proffit, of Mississippi, also three daughters Luberta Coldvin of Roswell, Anna McCroy of Ft. Huachuca, Arizona, and Marie Anderson of St. Louis, Missouri. Also, one brother, James Proffit of Mississippi. No funeral arrangement have been made pending word from relatives. Talmage Mortuary in charge.[1]

In July 1929, William Proffit went from Slavery to Freedom and died sovereign, as well as wealthy, in his Roswell, New Mexico home on South Michigan Street. Prophetic of a pending end, the Talmage Mortuary was owned by a businessman and Ku Klux Klan (KKK) Grand Dragon. Frank Talmage was in charge of William's funeral service and was a vocal leader in Roswell's KKK chapter. A few months after William's death, global financial markets collapsed and Blackdom's fate, as a town, blew away in the Dust Bowl of the 1930s.[2]

Fundamentally, Afro-Frontier*ism* mutes notions of a "rise and fall" and leans into the notion of Black history as part of a continuum. The Blackdom townsite scheme lasted about thirty years. Conceding the critique of Blackdom's brevity, the townsite was defunct shortly after the Great Depression began in the 1930s. Nevertheless, one must still grapple with the Blackdom Oil Company because the oil scheme continued into the post–World War II period.[3] At the risk of pedestrian conversation, one must ask why and/or how a few years of Black history are significant in a larger context of regional Indigenous histories that span time itself. The Black colonization continuum, informed by the notion of Afro-Frontierism, entitles one to view Blackdom with a new lens. Blackdomite society was a postscript of Exodusterism.

Exoduster narratives were imbued with strong inferences to Moses and the Israelites in search of promised land. Referencing the biblical book of Exodus oozes from short stories to brilliant dissertations. Afro-Frontierism suggests Black colonizers of the twentieth century were also spiritually motivated by the Book of Joshua, 1:1–3 (King James Version):

> 1 Now after the death of Moses the servant of the Lord it came
> to pass, that the Lord spake unto Joshua the son of Nun, Moses'
> minister, saying, 2 Moses my servant is dead; now therefore arise,
> go over this Jordan, thou, and all this people, unto the land which
> I do give to them, even to the children of Israel. 3 Every place that
> the sole of your foot shall tread upon, that have I given unto you, as
> I said unto Moses.[4]

Frank Boyer was often understood through the lens of Moses, who died before reaching the Promised Land.[5] Instead, the framework of Afro-Frontierism suggested, Francis Marion Boyer was inspired rather by the warrior Joshua. Frank was born free and, like Joshua, wasn't at his final destination. Frank and Joshua were on the edge of their "promised land." To possess God's promise for their lives, both had to cross the river Jordan. In Frank's case, locals called it the Pecos River.

A hundred years later, in the aftermath of a pandemic and on the verge of economic boom times, the current era echoes a not-so-distant past. As the postscript suggests, the Afro-Frontier thesis functions as a continuation, yet unique enough to pause and marvel at the organized improvisation of Africans in diaspora. The virtual community model was successfully employed by Blackdomites during the Roaring Twenties. The Blackdom Oil Company scheme sustained a minimum of two subsequent generations after 1929. Value in the intangible existence of African descendants in diaspora lack the "certainty" of a physical exploitation of old buildings and ruins. However, identifying the consciousness of Black folks in Chaves County reveals a lost story of generational wealth creation. Lost was the opportunity to replicate the successes and learn from the strategies Blackdomites used to endure and build until they began to thrive.

FRONTIER SOVEREIGN

In consonance with race thinking, the Pecos Valley region was styled as a Southern oasis. Does a "Black" person reckon with the dehumanizing public discourse, the internal discourse of Blackness and the descent into the abyss? Blackdom was an atonement for White impositions: it constituted "freedom." "Blackdom" was a conscious effort to employ freedom in search of sovereignty, a freedom to fully explore a spiritual striving. Ascent into Afrotopia was a sign of sovereign understandings of an existence in time and space along a messianic continuum. Provided *Plessy* was the law of the land, Black people had the right to maintain a segregated "exclusive Negro settlement" governed by the laws of a sovereign God who promised seed time and harvest time.

On the New Mexico side of the Pecos, however, there was no Jim Crow law enforcement in 1903. The new city of Roswell had streets, parks, and military installations named after states of the former Southern Confederacy as well as former military personnel. Jim Crow laws were not anchored in the local judicial system in the early 1900s because New Mexico was a territory. Black people felt the intentions of hegemonic society and responded with occupation of space between White New Mexican territorial racism and legalized racial segregation to enforce the impositions of White colonizers. The corporate veil of municipal governance in the US territory afforded Blackdomites collective land lordship that shielded them from a White superiority complex that hovered over socioeconomic transactions. The Blackdom Townsite Company's incorporation revealed Black intentionality as well as Blackdomite duality in their relationship to hegemonic society.

New Mexico's statehood loomed as Blackdomites feared a loss of autonomy as individual Black people. New Mexico's jurisdictional change from an incorporated federal territory to a US state of the union forced Black people to abide by local laws created by local people. Statehood threatened not only the Black body in Chaves County but also their children's future. Moreover, Black folks had little to protect their spiritual striving once the shift in power occurred. New Mexico's pending statehood was a backdrop for Blackdomites. The conditions of American Blackness were less adversarial in Southeastern New Mexico, but Black people were locked into a permanent underclass. A new set of White colonizers increased the social projection of supremacy in Whiteness. Building a Black town was one of the few significant opportunities to change the familial and social life trajectory by embracing the vagaries of the desert.

Early Blackdomites embraced the reality of America's racial nadir and the promise of God-like sovereignty. Also, Blackdomites maintained a collective notion of a spiritual kingdom of God undergirded by biblical prophecy. Blackdom was an insurance against local invasions on their God-given sovereignty. Blackdom was motivated by speculative future profits. Behind the corporate veil, Black people increased their individual and communal capacity to achieve Afrotopia as they transformed into frontier sovereigns. In the Borderlands, Blackdom was a story of people under the conditions of American Blackness, who devised a legal way to achieve God's sovereignty. Full manifestation of Blackdom included physical and spiritual autonomy; land and wealth accumulation were a few of the opportunities to directly experience God's promise. The Afrocentric autonomy project opened new and profound opportunities beyond simple profit-taking. In the Afro-Frontier of Chaves County, an all-Black municipality elevated believers/doers to sovereigns.

Blackdomites envisioned a 10,000-person county of Black folks. According to the Articles of Incorporation, the Blackdom Thirteen bought stock to form the company. In 1903, the Blackdom Townsite Company became one of the newest institutions within the Black community of Chaves County. However, unlike for a church or a school, the effort necessary to be successful required belief and, eventually, a lifestyle change. Half of the Blackdom Thirteen were in a position to develop a new town from the ground up. In the case of 1903 Blackdom, it seems as though there was little to no commitment from its founders. Four were absent from public accounts such as census records but remained with the thirteen names on the Articles: Charles W. Clifton, Benjamin Harrison, George White, and Joseph Cook. Although the Blackdom project had thirteen men listed on its public documents, there was no record of anyone homesteading explicitly for the purpose of building Blackdom before 1909.

The objectives were as follows:

> Article III
> To establish a Negro colony and to found and erect the town of Blackdom, and to lay off the lands covered by said town into a townsite under the laws of the Territory of New Mexico and to lay out additions thereto, and to plat said townsite and additions into blocks, lots, streets, alleys, avenues, commons, parks and public grounds and to own, hold, sell, and convey said lots and blocks and improve the same.
>
> To purchase, sell, improve, cultivate and colonize lands in connection with the matter mentioned in paragraph 1 of these purposes.
>
> To purchase, build, erect, construct and operate one or more irrigation plants by means of a system of artesian wells, or appropriating the now unappropriated waters of any natural stream in the County of Chaves and Territory of New Mexico and the construction of reservoirs, canals, ditches and pipes for the purposes of irrigation and reclamation of lands, and the sale of waters and water rights in connection therewith.
>
> To maintain and establish irrigated farms and to handle, sell and dispose of the products thereof.
>
> To establish a system of education among the inhabitants of the town of Blackdom and surrounding country and to improve the health, welfare and prosperity of such inhabitants.
>
> In general it is proposed to gain control of a large body of land in the County of Chaves and Territory of New Mexico under the laws of the United States of America and there to establish and maintain a colony of Negroes by means of the cultivation of crops, the growing

> of town and settlements and the general improvement of the inhabitants of such colony; to build, erect and equip schoolhouses, colleges, churches and various educational and religious institutions for the improvement and upbuilding of the moral and mental condition of said colony.

Notable in Article IV, Blackdom Townsite Company's incorporation documents, is "Capital Stock: That the amount of capital stock of this corporation shall be ten thousand dollars, which shall be divided into five thousand shares of the par value of two dollars each."

THE BLACKDOM THIRTEEN

On September 5, 1903, Blackdomites established their intentions as a company and invested. The collective projections of Blackdom encouraged Blackdomites to advance the cause. Black folks, who were a permanent underclass in Roswell, became co-founders of a new "Exclusive Negro Settlement." Under the guise of municipality, through incorporation of the Blackdom Townsite Company, Blackdomites became rulers of their own domain—from second-class citizenship to land lordship.

There were Black people who homesteaded before Blackdom was an idea in Chaves County. Incorporation served as a declaration of frontier sovereignty for all who believed and solidified the authority of Black folks to project their new reality. According to Article VI, "Provided however, that until such town is established the business of said company shall be transacted in the town of Roswell, in the County of Chaves and Territory of New Mexico." Blackdomites did not wait for the town to be built before they declared their autonomy; again, belief was all that was necessary to be a Blackdomite. Thirteen Black men signed Blackdom Townsite Company's articles of incorporation. Women were significant in a Black folks–centered microcosm of a patriarchal hegemonic society. Amongst themselves as town's people, they negotiated their worth and position. The newest influx of Black people motivated the earlier wave of migrants to consider township. Separate-and-equal, Black people were allowed to fully engage the macro marketplace behind the veil of legal authority. The investment of capacity, time, money, and resources in service to the idea of Blackdom was a gamble on rains that often didn't come.

Burrel Dickerson

Five of the Blackdom Thirteen ascended to Afrotopia in the form of homestead patents, connected to the idea of Blackdom. Six of them were homesteaders by 1908. Burrel Dickerson, however, was a homesteader prior to the establishment of Blackdom. Isaac Jones, Charles Childress, John Boyer, Frank Boyer, and Daniel Keys all homesteaded on 160 acres of land, the maximum allotment at the time. The treasurer and co-founder of Blackdom Townsite Company, Burrel Dickerson, completed his final homestead proof on August 4, 1890. Isaac and Charles were residents in Roswell and watched the town grow exponentially—economically and socially—around Burrel's quarter of a square mile of the city. Burrel financially benefited from the growth and served as a model for the Blackdomite homestead class. He was also proof of the potential for conversion on desert prairies into power, capital, and sovereignty.

Burrel Dickerson had become an early homesteader in the development of the newly incorporated City of Roswell that transitioned from a village on April 25, 1903. Possibly, Isaac Jones was inspired by these events; he began his homestead paperwork the same month. Vice President Jones homesteaded about fifteen miles south of the city on land adjacent to Highway 285. The roads and the nearest train station in newly incorporated Dexter, New Mexico, led 200 miles north in a direct route to Santa Fe. From Blackdom to the territorial capital and home of the Montezuma Freemason Grand Lodge of New Mexico, Blackdomites had direct access to power in a world colonized by Freemasons, railroads, and modern communication. Another possible catalyst for Isaac Jones's action (as well as the collective decision to locate Afrotopia and themselves in the general area twenty miles south of Roswell), in January 1903, Dexter incorporated as a village. Chaves County was bustling with activity and in September 1903, Blackdomites incorporated.

On October 1, 1903, the *Santa Fe New Mexican* followed up the story of Blackdom's incorporation with an in-depth article, "The Blackdom Townsite," subtitled, "An Exclusive Negro Settlement to be Located in Southern Part of Chaves County":

> A town and settlement exclusively for negroes are being organized in the southern part of Chaves County, within the artesian belt, some few miles from Pecos valley railroad. The promoters of this settlement expect to settle 10,000 people at one time, so as to avoid the enactment of a special law by Congress, debarring anyone but colored settlers from certain townships.
>
> The settlement promoters style themselves the Blackdom Townsite company, and May 1, 1904, has been decided upon as the opening day. The officers of the company which is capitalized at $10,000, are F. M. Boyer, A.M., president; Rev. I. N. Jones, vice president: Professor D. G. Keyes [*sic*], secretary; and Burrell [*sic*] Dickerson, treasurer. The address of President Boyer in Dexter, N.M.
>
> While artesian wells are to form the basin of the water supply for the town site, the company expects to operate a large number of irrigation pumps. With pumping system in charge of expert machinists and engineers.
>
> The president of the company has written to the secretary of the bureau of immigration asking for 500 or more of the Chaves County pamphlets. He also wished information regarding pumping systems, and the pumps best adapted to irrigation in New Mexico.
>
> The company is also desires [*sic*] of securing concessions from the railroads on which their colonists will have to travel. Most of the colonists will come from the South and bring with them cattle and swine. A tanning factory is also to be erected on the Blackdom townsite.[6]

From Santa Fe, newspapers across the colonized US echoed Blackdom's Afrotopic striving across America. Blackdomites announced officers who represented the institution.

Isaac Jones

Beyond notions of a US trans-Appalachian West and the centrality of the Mississippi River, in the Borderlands, Mexico's northern frontier and the Rio Grande River were more helpful tools to orient Blackdom's narrative. Isaac Jones was born in North Carolina during the US Civil War. In the postbellum period, Isaac migrated to the Borderlands as the US empire lurched westward to establish state and territorial corporatocracies. Isaac Jones went to Texas where he met Mollie, who was ten years younger than he. Mollie agreed to marry in the late 1890s; they had a son and moved to Roswell.[7] The resettlement of the Jones family was significant because they transitioned from a Jim Crow Texas to the New Mexico territory. Although the Pecos River was not a recognized border, occupation on the New Mexico side signified in hegemonic society a border that released Black people from the recognizable White supremacist oppression tactics that oozed from incorporated states and local governments.

The Jones family settled on the New Mexican side of the Pecos River, in Roswell. Provided one was willing to stay in the servant class, a Black person had a relatively good chance there to grow old and, possibly, support and raise a family. As a minister, Isaac harbored a longing for Afrotopia as well as income and residual profits. In the time before he was introduced to Blackdom, as a literate Black man in his early forties, he found the city life adequate in the furtherance of its ancestral trajectory from slavery to relative freedom. Behind the corporate veil of Blackdom Townsite Company, Isaac repositioned himself in hegemonic society from colonized/free to colonizer/sovereign. As a Roswellian, Isaac was free to participate in a stable society. As a Blackdomite, Isaac employed his freedom in the creation of a society promised by God to those who believe in the kingdom. Isaac's beliefs outweighed the enormity of proving up a desert homestead, in part because he found a cohort of similar thinking people. Once "Blackdom" was introduced at the intersection of ambitious Black folks, all who believed became more resilient and bolder in their striving as Blackdom became a matter of faith in a perceived reality.

As vice president of the Blackdom Townsite Company, Isaac Jones was the highest-ranking member to build a homestead before and during the inception of the company. Jones's existence prior to the advent of the company was typical of Black people in the region. He was born in the South and migrated to the Borderlands, where he married. Living on Kentucky Avenue in Roswell in 1900, Jones was a cook while his wife Mollie worked at home taking care of their six-year-old son.[8]

Isaac Jones began his homesteading process in April 1903, but homesteading required significant investment of a few thousand dollars with no guarantee of success. Without significant cash reserves, Jones did not have any margin for error, building his homestead with his family in tow. Making a mistake in the choice of crops or any aspect of homesteading would lead to a yearlong march toward economic disaster with very little means of recovery. For several months, he made little progress on his homestead while still working in Roswell.

Charles C. Childress

Charles Childress was one of the Blackdom Thirteen about whom little is known. Charles was, however, the only Blackdom Townsite Company co-founder to begin a homestead patent between the 1903 incorporation and May 1904 scheduled open. A rustic bourgeoisie standardized. The highest Afrotopic achievement was a land patent and membership in Blackdom's society. Keeping pace with Isaac Jones, Charles Childress succeeded early and completed his homestead in October 1905.[9] Blackdomite society separated into those with patents and those looking to do so in the future. The Chaves County Afrotopia developed a third tier in its social strata to include non-homesteaders.

Roswell resident Charles Childress, co-founder of the Blackdom Townsite Company, was mature in age with his peak laborer days behind him. Nevertheless, on October 2, 1905, in less than three years, he completed his first homestead a mile east of highway 285 at Township 013S - Range 025E, Section 24, in Chaves County. Childress's land was half of the way between Dexter, New Mexico, train station and the Blackdom Townsite official location. Nine years passed before Blackdom had a town square, and Blackdomites all faced different circumstances from age to capacity. Through the Blackdomite system, their united consciousness bore increasingly more fruit each season. However, between 1903 and 1909, the steep learning curve and harsh homesteading conditions may nearly have prevented the first few families from following through with Afrotopia. In the early years, Blackdom was almost a lost cause.

Childress was the only member to file a homestead patent between September 1903 and May 1904 in the afterglow of the Blackdom Townsite announcement. Childress built on his homestead and improved it enough to complete the final stage of the patent process in 1905. Although Charles Childress was the only one of the Blackdom Thirteen immediately to homestead after 1903, it was not to build Blackdom; it was to build "Blackdom."

John A. Boyer

On August 16, 1907, John Boyer became the first in his family to achieve frontier sovereignty. John was born under the major institutions of US slavery. At the age of 51, he became a homesteader along with wife Pinkie and three sons Porter (11), Ethon (12), and Berry (15). John was born and raised in Pelham, Georgia, on the plantation of Elias Boyer at the start of the US Civil War. Following his younger brother Frank, John migrated to Chaves County and began a life in Roswell, establishing a household on South Main Street. After completing his homestead, he had a ranch in Blackdom at Township 014S - Range 024E, Section 14, in Chaves County and a life in the hub city. His dual reality, as part of Roswell's servant class, reflected little of his existence as co-founder of an "Exclusive Negro Colony." His postscript to freedom, separate and equal, set a standard in the Boyer dynasty that followed.

Daniel Keys

Daniel Keys married into the Boyer family, to Frank's sister. Daniel and Frank homesteaded on two contiguous 160-acre lots, the equivalent of one-half of a square mile. The president of the Blackdom Townsite Company, Frank Boyer, did not seek to begin the homesteading process until 1906, but he did use the name of the somewhat famed Blackdom for his own personal interests before that time. On June 11, 1908, Daniel and Frank completed the homestead process and lived in Afrotopia on land near the Pecos River as well as the Dexter train station. In 1909, all major officers in the Blackdom Townsite Company were landlords in a generalized area. However, growth and public entrance decelerated as the rigors of desert toil dissuaded those with little capacity and/or resources to endure. If drought conditions were not enough to discourage the mostly Southern farmer class of Black migrants to Blackdom, the time constraints and bureaucracy broke the will of unbelievers.

Charles Thompson

Charles (Charlie/Charley) Thompson signed the Blackdom Townsite Company's Articles of Incorporation. In 1903, Thompson was new to Chaves County and a newlywed; "Blackdom" was a chance for him to build something substantial. With no children, Thompson was a prime candidate for developing "Blackdom." Living in Roswell, Thompson and his wife Emma, who was a seamstress, had the opportunity to sacrifice one of their incomes to build a desert homestead. Still, they chose not to do so. It was not until the revival of the Blackdom idea that the Thompsons established a homestead near the future townsite. Charlie's patience proved to be a virtue when he homesteaded at Township 013S - Range 025E, Section 12 in Chaves County's 13th Draw on January 23, 1914, in the midst of Blackdom's revival period.

James Jackson

Another co-founder of the Blackdom Townsite Company, James Jackson, was in his sixties when he invested in the idea of "Blackdom." Jackson, however, was not a prime candidate expected to invest fully due to his advanced age. Because Chaves County was mostly desert prairies, one required significant investment, along with initiative, to drill a well for irrigation among other investments in livestock, feed, and building materials for living quarters. Jackson spent his life as a laborer and could hardly maintain the rigors of desert homesteading for an extended period.

Albert Hubert

For literate Texan and co-founder of the Blackdom Townsite Company Albert Hubert, homesteading was "iffy." Hubert began his time in Chaves County around 1900 when he was "about 30." Even though Hubert had a family of his own, in census records he was also identified as the "servant" of the Travis Ellis family. Travis Ellis was a 29-year-old railroad auditor from Kentucky. Travis's 27-year-old wife Maude was born in Indiana but migrated from Kentucky as well. In 1900, with the help of Hubert, Maude worked from home taking care of two daughters under the age of ten.

Hubert, like most Black people in the county, was securely in the servant class for his entire existence in Roswell. He lived the majority of his years on East Third Street, growing his family every three to five years. When Hubert became a member of the Blackdom Thirteen in 1903, his family consisted of his 20-year-old wife Pearl, his 2-year-old daughter Sadee, and a 9-year-old daughter Bernice from a previous relationship.

By 1920, Hubert's family comprised of his wife and six children: Bernice (24), Juanita (18), Linwood (14), Valerie (12), Burt (10), and Mattie (7). From 1900 through 1920, he remained a cook as he added to his family. There were very few opportunities for him to change his economic status over the course of his tenure, until the signing of the

Blackdom Townsite Company's Articles of Incorporation in 1903.[10]

Building the town of Blackdom was an opportunity that required a tremendous amount of work before yielding a profit. Full investment in Blackdom required that one homestead. Hubert never homesteaded and well into his forties was still a cook. For a brief moment, however, the Ellis family cook became a co-founder and board member of New Mexico's only all-Black townsite company. Nevertheless, Hubert decided to continue focusing his attention on providing for his family rather than investing in the Black colonization venture.

In 1920, Hubert was a 48-year-old hotel cook still living on East Third Street. In 1903, Albert Hubert was one of thirteen founders of the Blackdom Townsite Company who didn't fully invest and stayed "a servant" his whole life. According to three decades of census records, Albert was a stable head of household in Chaves County, New Mexico. Abiding was no easy feat. Albert's life strategy sustained him as a Black man at the chaotic intersection of Mexico's northern frontier and America's western frontier, as borders crossed people.

Blackdomites occupied space virtually by maintaining a home "in town" and proving up a homestead connected to the idea of Blackdom. At the will of the people, dual existence allowed Blackdom to assemble, disassemble, and reassemble. Blackdom's nimble concept allowed the township to weather times of tumult and thrive in boom times. In 1914, Blackdom Townsite's original forty-acre plot was officially patented, but the process began in 1909 after a lackluster attempt in 1903. The homestead class dictated Blackdom Township's agenda; meanwhile, the townsite languished for years while they struggled to produce a sovereign life on subsistence dry farming. Many Black folks had to leave their families on homesteads for long periods of time to make ends meet. Albert's side hustle in the city became his main hustle, and Blackdom Township lost him to a consistent paycheck as well as the responsibility to his blossoming family.

CHAPTER 4

AFROTOPIA

BLACKDOM, DU BOIS, AND DESCENT INTO AFROTOPIA

The Afrotopia referred to in this chapter (the first of three parts) begins in a "state" of surrealism influenced by the omnipresence of W. E. B. Du Bois's 1903 *The Souls of Black Folk* and a July 1920 letter written to him from Ruth Loomis Skeen, a White woman.[1] She happened to live twenty miles south of Blackdom at the start of Blackdom's transition during the Harlem Renaissance. At the time, Du Bois was editor of *The Crisis* magazine, aimed at the betterment of Black folks as well as an outlet for the NAACP. Blackdom (an Afrotopic paradigm) was officially platted as a town in May 1920 and further matured as an investment that included oil royalties. Blackdom was a real place with a tangible means of expression that expounded on personally held notions of Afrotopia. Ontologically, Blackdomites exceeded the goals of Black liberation theology as well as Ethiopianism between 1903 and 1920. On the precipice of boom times during an age often referred to as the Roaring Twenties, Ruth Loomis Skeen's letter to Du Bois therefore functions as a testimonial of Blackdomites' successful articulation of Afrotopia, a tangible means of Black expression, during a period of Black Renaissance.

Employing Du Bois's work, in a surrealistic conversation with Skeen's observation, this chapter details Blackdom's first decade while maintaining Blackdom's full trajectory expressed in Skeen's letter. Blackdomites could not predict the weather or the events of the next day; it was inconceivable that they could foresee what would happen over the course of the first two decades. In part due to the miseducation of Black folks, we must enter Blackdom's Afrotopia behind the Du Boisian "veil of Blackness" knowing that Blackdomites had a belief that a good man's steps were ordered by God. In short, according to their belief system, provided one was willing to apply Christian as well as Masonic ideals and concepts to the collective experience of Blackdom, God would bless them for their faithful endurance. Without knowing the future, Blackdomites assumed success was inevitable after the trials and tragedy of desert homesteading guaranteed by God's promise. In the Borderlands, Blackdomites had faith in divine sovereignty that was sure to come.

Blackdomites believed in a collective spiritual and daily toil. Ruth Skeen wrote to W. E. B. Du Bois in 1920:

> I have greatly enjoyed the sample copies of "The Crisis" and if you will send me two or three copies of the Brownie Book [*The Brownies' Book*, a literary magazine aimed at African American children]. I will take them, with the samples of the Crisis and visit a colored settlement near here and endeavour to secure subscriptions for your good magazine.
>
> There are not many colored people in this part of our state although we have many Mexicans and the race feeling against them is quite bitter. They are not allowed to enter a white barber shop nor to eat in a white man's eating place.
>
> However, in the northern part of the state they own a good deal of property and are well educated and hold positions of trust and honor. Our Governor is a Spanish-American born in old Mexico.

> Of course, historically, the Spanish people have a perfect right here and there are persons in the state possessing a fair attitude toward them—but they are only what [English writer John] Ruskin calls "a little group of wise hearts in a wilderness of fools."
>
> Near here is a settlement of Negroes, a little town called "Blackdom," consisting of farmers who have wrenched every bit of good out of our bitter soil. They are quiet, good citizens and molest nobody. They have had little chance for the cultural things of life and I believe they would welcome an opportunity to take your papers and magazines. Of course, they may already know about them. They have a little school and a Church.
>
> At any rate, I will be glad to go over in my car and take them the books. I have lived among Negroes all of my life, have had them in my home as helpers, and known them very well, but I had never, until going to California, lived where they were not segregated.[2]

Thus, according to Ruth Loomis Skeen, Blackdomites appeared in full expression of Afrotopia in 1920.

Unbound by the geography of the New York–based Black Renaissance movement and her ethnic background, Ruth Skeen was a poet of Irish heritage who also went by the pen name Rheba Cain. She lived in places from California to New York and, although she was a "White woman," per her understanding, Black folks maintained their souls and knew how to express themselves. In an apparent attempt to "negro-tize" her name as an author, in a 1929 issue of *The Crisis* magazine, located in New York on Fifth Avenue, she published "Dark Lover."[3] Cognizant of the time in which she existed, Skeen's minstrel expression of her soul in poems from a position on the Black side of town highlights a slightly veiled Black space difficult to experience on the other side of the proverbial veil. The two-ness was used for all who engage in the practice.

Blackdom was an "in-between" (frontier) space in the Mexican–US Borderlands where Black people quarantined to engage their duality to achieve Afrotopia. Wilson Moses's notion of Afrotopia informs how one might imagine a society built from a singular Black intersectional messianic consciousness and helps interpret the documented activities of Blackdomites in the midst of a dual reality.[4] Moses tracked Afrocentrism as well as anti-modernism and notions of utopia from the 1700s through the nineteenth century. Also important to this study, Moses's work *The Golden Age of Black Nationalism, 1850–1925* helped contextualize postbellum Blackness in early twentieth century America.[5] Moses's works illuminate the centrality of back-to-Africa schemes and bring into focus the new Blackdom narrative trajectory, shifting from a freedom model to a sovereignty model. Mostly untold, the history of Blackdom disrupts the tricultural narrative.

BLACKDOM'S INTERSECTION AND THE "OLE" TRICULTURAL NARRATIVE

The *Albuquerque Journal* published a February 14, 1965, segment whose headline read "50 Years Ago." One must take into account the Pecos Valley region's Confederate past and White supremist–led efforts as well as the article's being written in the 1960s during significant politicization of human rights. It depicted a traveler to Artesia, twenty miles south of Blackdom and the same place from which Ruth Loomis Skeen wrote her letter:

> Artesia —A short time ago the Negro preacher from Blackdom, a Negro settlement in Chaves County, came to Artesia to solicit funds for a new church. He received a liberal response to his plea for donations and went home well pleased with the consideration given him, but there are no Negroes residing in this town. Artesia is the only town of any size in New Mexico where colored race is absolutely barred out.[6]

The piece written in 1965 was meant to reflect Blackdom fifty years prior, around 1915. How does one reconcile Blackdom's reality for some and not others?

As we focus on significance, success or failure hinges on one's perception. Newly discovered documentation challenges a pedestrian view of New Mexicanity as a triad of Indigenous, Spanish, and White people. The tricultural narrative germinated in a unique space colonized by people of a White consciousness that helped erase histories. New Mexicanity bent toward White supremacy, over time. Evident of the complicated space, however, White colonizers were not the unique source of hegemonic power. The newest wave of colonization at the turn of the twentieth century, in the so-called "North American" continental interior, collided with inhabitants conditioned to resist. Indigenous and Native peoples resisted long enough that White colonizers relented to racialization and creation of more White-ish people.[7]

In September 1903, Chaves County's economic surge had undergone a wave of business incorporations after regional large infrastructure projects (described in chapter 2). Thirteen Black men signed the Blackdom Townsite Company's articles of incorporation and were able to function as businessmen. In so doing, Blackdomites veiled themselves from the vagaries of a society beholden to White supremacy as well as physicality. At the turn of the twentieth century, what had become the US territory of New Mexico was in transition to statehood and a final annexation of Indigenous lands. The White supremacist violence extended beyond bloody battles and massacre; systematic corporatocracy within the homestead processes shifted borders and people as a perpetual reminder of the ongoing horrors in reservation life.

Hosting the prior Spanish colonizer, Indigenous and Native peoples had to endure a new wave of English-speaking colonizers and a new colonization system that had to expand to include their bodies in the underclasses.[8] Specifically, the US racialization process to create new levels of Whiteness from Indigenous and Native bodies provided social space for Black ambitions to fully mature: separate-but-equal.[9] African descendants as they were, Blackdomites colonized in the midst of a collision at the intersection of Mexico's northern frontier and the United States' western frontier. Black and other colonizer groups used homesteading to benefit from the displacement and dismantling of Indigenous and Native communities.

In the case of Black folks, New Mexico's statehood ensured increased impositions at the hands of people in Chaves County dominated by the "White" consciousness. The shift of power, from federal to local jurisdictions in New Mexico, was important in the Blackdom narrative as a Black homesteader motivator. White people were occupied with transforming Indigenous and Native People into a racialized something (close to Whiteness), allowing Black folks to exist as separate-and-equal under the law.

THE LOST YEARS, 1903–1909

Consider this section's title "The Lost Years" as ambiguous because of our shift in focus to highlight significance on the "Black side of town." Depending on one's perspective, the early struggle of Blackdomites was both lost and found: lost in the notion of the old world that Black folks understood, and found because the town proceeded to grow through the Great Depression. Lost was the Black poverty in a White-dominated society. Through the lens of the standard Black narrative, freedom to exist as the permanent underclass was lost in the Blackdomite quest for frontier sovereignty. Early Blackdomites fell short of "large" land acquisitions to build a town, and few were able to prove up a homestead so that many were lost to "the struggle." Blackdom, however, endured as a desirable idea long enough to function as insurance against New Mexico's imminent statehood.

In September 1903, the Kokomo, Indiana, *Daily Tribune* (on page 7) reported, "Organization of Blackdom."[10] Black folks who had recently migrated to the incorporated state of Indiana endured a summer of White violence. Blackdomites focused on Indiana as the entire US was exposed to the creation of Blackdom Townsite Company. Blackdom was an autonomy project specifically designed by people in Chaves County, who had the privilege of little to no Jim Crow law enforcement in the US Territory. Folklore about Blackdom emphasizes the importance of White violence but, facing little to no White violence, Blackdom was built by people who reached a place of relative sovereignty and invited others to join. Blackdom's early years appeared *lost* as Black homesteaders attempted to adjust to the steep learning curve of desert farming. Blackdomites maximized individual capacity with community support, apprenticeships, and host families for better integration of new immigrants over time.

The Eubank family's initial exposure to the Afro-Frontier town Blackdom scheme is unclear, but homestead records document their journey in Afrotopia. Nurtured in messianic colonization ideals, Black folks building a town on hard-to-irrigate Mescalero Apache Reservation desert land required a significant amount of imagination and faith. Significant in the story of Blackdomites, the homestead process functioned as a day-by-day and year-by-year standardized process to measure one's progress. Advantageous to the Blackdom scheme, homesteading ensured there were actions to take, planning to manage, and a clear phase of execution uniformly understood by all of the illuminated observers.

In 1903, Blackdom's incorporation was advertised throughout the United States. Associated Press outlets echoed from the *Santa Fe New Mexican*. More than likely, Crutcher Eubank (the family patriarch) harbored colonization intentions as part of his training in Liberation Theology as a minister from Kentucky, and was exposed through his network of ministers, many of whom were Freemasons. In 1904, the lack of a "massive" influx of immigrants and migrants signaled Blackdomites' slow ascension into Afrotopia. Credible in the minds of those with a similar consciousness, Blackdom maintained a dual reality and often contracted to only exist in the tangible world, on paper, in signed notarized incorporation documents. On an archetypical Afrotopic trajectory, the Eubank family narrative reveals profound significance in understanding Blackdom better. After a century has passed, descendants continue to own land in what was Blackdom.

1904 MAY: BLACKDOM'S RECEPTION

The Eubank family endured slavery and the failure of Reconstruction and found opportunity in the 1896 US Supreme Court decision in *Plessy*. Black people were granted lawful separation from White people. In 1904, Crutcher Eubank's Afrotopic vision of separate and equal under the law was realized when the family immigrated across the Pecos River and into Chaves County. The Eubank family's Black nationalism was born on a slave plantation. Over time the Black church defined a sovereignty provision in frontier territorial space.

Blackdom's grand opening in May 1904 fell short of physical expectations. However, the significance of "Blackdom" (the idea) increased as a counter hegemonic balance to ensure their future sovereignty. According to the Texas *Hereford Reporter*, under the headline "New Mexico to Have a Nigger Town," Blackdom was set to "open May 1, 1904, at which time the promoters propose to locate 10,000 negroes."[11]

The Eubank family was a part of the first wave of Black migrants to arrive in Chaves County for the purpose of building an all-Black municipality. Frank, Ella, and the Boyer family became intimately acquainted with the Eubank family when the Boyers hosted them for a year. The Boyers homesteaded in Dexter near the train station where the Eubank family would have arrived. Significantly, they were all on the west side of the Pecos River, which signaled the end of Jim Crow laws in the region.

1905 EUBANK FAMILY

Mostly influenced by the desire to engage the more popular notion of Blackdom, I wrote a 3,000-word essay that highlighted Blackdom's "lost years" featuring the Eubank Family. Accurate in my assessment of the family's first year as homesteaders and second year in Chaves County, I wrote, "The Eubank family was faithful, consistent, and hard-working, but they sowed seeds in the right place at the wrong time and reaped little harvest for their toil."[12] In the spring 2021 issue of New Mexico State Department of Cultural Affairs' 107-year-old *El*

Palacio magazine, I was preoccupied with establishing a basic narrative trajectory for people who were new to the idea of Afrotopia. The Eubank family had an appreciation for education, as shown by the accomplishments of granddaughter Grace, who earned a degree from Lincoln University in Missouri.[13]

According to my original interpretations, the Eubank family embodied the era of loss. After further excavation, what appeared as failure may have been an experimental plan unique to the region, time, and space. Blackdom was located 200 miles west of Lubbock, Texas. There, William Curry Holden published his study, "Agriculture on the Spur Ranch," at Texas Technological College in 1932. Holden examined the experimental ranch "located in Garza, Kent, Crosby, and Dickens counties, [that] was owned and operated from 1885 to 1907 by a British syndicate with a home office in London."[14] Holden's 1932 study focused on Northwest Texas. Holden's work reaffirmed the region's global agricultural economic potential as early as 1879. Removing the illusion of borders, Northwest Texas included "Eastern New Mexico" or "Little Texas." During the Eubank family's experiment with Afrotopia, they also participated in regional experimental agricultural techniques.

Only recently had I become aware of Blackdom's significance in the region's agricultural trajectory at the turn of the twentieth century. I participated in an online discussion panel with Janice Dunahoo, archivist and community columnist; Geni Flores, coordinator of bilingual and TESOL (Teaching English to Speakers of Other Languages) education at Eastern New Mexico University; and Maya Allen, a PhD student in biology at the University of New Mexico who focuses on how plants cope with environmental heterogeneity and a particular underlying mechanism, phenotypic plasticity—the ability for a single genotype to differentially express alternative phenotypes based on the environment. For the New Mexico Humanities Council public humanities program "Starting Conversations: we all presented our perspective on Blackdom's significance.[15] Maya Allen's work suggests my initial conclusion about whether or not the Eubank family was short-sighted. My simplistic notions of the Eubank family, and specifically Crutcher's faith, colored my perspective when I wrote, "He misread the warm-weather plant that early growth was steady, but his leap of faith was inefficient."[16]

An elementary survey of regional botanical history reveals a legacy of experiment in the region. In a humble attempt to reintroduce the Eubank family in this Afrotopic narrative, I return to their use of kaffir corn. By most measurements of successful farming on desert prairies, the Eubank family's first year of homesteading appeared disastrous as they planted kaffir corn, a warm-weather crop, in a winter ground. Belonging to the sorghum family, the plant grows to between five to seven feet and was a native crop from Southern Africa.[17] Kaffir corn was an experimental foreign crop for the region. The Eubank family therefore was a part of the region's period of agricultural experimentation.

In migrating from Kentucky into the Afro-Frontier space of Blackdom, the Eubank family joined other Blackdomites in an unincorporated agricultural community. Inspired by the notion of Blackdom articulated in the Blackdom Townsite Company's Articles of Incorporation, Crutcher Eubank began the family homestead patent on October 9, 1906.[18] The Eubank family was hardworking and in their first year focused on producing seeds of the experimental kaffir corn. In all likelihood, the Eubank family harvested an exponential number of seeds relative to what they planted.[19] The value created by seed production had the potential to reap enormous reward for the start-up homestead.

Experiments proved that if a sufficient stand was secured in the first planting in a cold-winter ground, significantly more cultivation was needed than if sown in a warm ground. The Eubank family was keenly aware of the socioeconomics in Chaves County and could live relatively free in Roswell as part of the Southern-style servant class. Instead, they chose the struggle for sovereignty that rested on seed production in their first year as homesteaders. Crutcher systematically submitted to the

Blackdomite pattern of leaving one's family to raise capital working as a laborer on nearby homesteads or in nearby cities to subsist during the time of the agricultural experiments. Possibly in the bartering economy that developed, Blackdomites were eager to help the Eubank family through their early years in New Mexico's southern frontier.

1906 THE BOYER, EUBANK, RAGSDALE, AND HAGERMAN FAMILIES

In 1906, the Boyer and Eubank families homesteaded in Chaves County. At the time, Frank Boyer was Blackdom Townsite Company's president. Legitimizing further investment in New Mexico's southern region, in 1906, Herbert J. Hagerman, James Hagerman's son, was federally appointed to the seventeenth territorial governorship of New Mexico out of the capital Santa Fe 200 miles north on highway 285. James and Herbert used their tremendous influence to solidify Chaves County's place as a regional economic driver of exponential growth in southeastern New Mexico.

Blackdom had a slow progression, and the new settler families brought with them talent and fresh understanding of the potential for generational wealth creation. From Mississippi in 1906, and hosted by the Boyer family, the Ragsdale family settled as homesteaders. Blackdom's emergence as an oil-producing town during the Harlem Renaissance was enhanced by Clinton Ragsdale's engineering background specialty in pumping.[20] In his mid-30s when he began a life in Chaves County, Clinton arrived from Mississippi in 1906 and began his homestead in 1907, living in a tent.[21] Frank Boyer's development as a minister, a former Buffalo Soldier, and a Freemason served Blackdomite society. Frank functioned as a foundational intersection for ministers such as Crutcher Eubank and Freemasons like Clinton Ragsdale whose engineering expertise became a vital resource when Blackdomite society shifted in 1920 to drilling for oil instead of water.

Little coordination took place after 1903 in Blackdom's progression except within small units and families. For example, Frank Boyer and his brother-in-law Daniel Keys began homestead patents near the town of Dexter, New Mexico (five miles west of Blackdom) on the same day in 1906. Contributing to the confusion of when Blackdom began, Frank, who was often considered the single most important leader, spent his first three years building capital and renting land. As the system developed, homesteading in Blackdom became more systematic and predictive. However, lost in the process were early-wave Blackdomite children such as James Eubank, who was one of the first teachers in Blackdom school with little to no desire to homestead.

1907 JOHN BOYER HOMESTEAD

Boyer family allies, specifically Judge Freeman, started migrating out of New Mexico. The judge retired to British Columbia, where he had invested in the lumber industry.[22] Judge Freeman fully withdrew from the New Mexico bar in early 1908, when Frank Boyer completed his first homestead patent. Formally, Frank Boyer had declared his sovereignty from jobs outside of Blackdom and focused more on the development of Blackdom's town square.

Although John Boyer, Frank's brother, completed the first family homestead in 1907, collectively, Blackdomites had no land directly anchoring the existence of the town. Instead, Blackdomites operated as townspeople without a town. Many Blackdomites began individual homesteads before 1909. Blackdomites had an insatiable appetite for land and absorbed what they were legally allowed.

On the Eve of New Mexico's statehood, John Boyer homesteaded for a second time under the Enlargement Act and grew his landholding by 320 acres. John had endured life as a child on a slave plantation in Georgia, and at the age of 54 in 1910, he had reached sovereignty and was in the midst of growing generational wealth. His first land patent was granted on August 16, 1907, and set the frantic pace of the Boyers' land grab in Blackdom's commons. When New Mexico became a state, John had a homestead patent in a municipality he helped build, called Blackdom. He also owned a home in the city on South Main.

Meanwhile, in 1907, Crutcher Eubank broke ground on two acres of his land, which yielded little. In the 1908 growing season, Crutcher planted more kaffir corn for a total of four acres. By 1909, he broke ground on another two acres, planting corn, beans, potatoes, and other garden products over the six acres. In 1910, Crutcher replanted on the acreage of previous years. In 1911, Crutcher prayed, and the rains came to relieve the region of droughts.

A growing hostility towards non-White people was reflected in headlines and articles devoted to perpetual racialization in Borderlands regions. As noted in a Las Vegas (New Mexico) *Daily Optic* 1907 article entitled "Negro Shot at the Castaneda," the "third cook attempts to kill colored bartender" Will Henderson in Las Vegas. According to the article, the "injured man receives bullet in left thigh—both placed in jail—coon trouble and fired first."[23] The colloquialism "coon," short for zip coon, derived from a minstrel caricature of Black people, common in popular media, meant to dehumanize.[24]

1908 HOMESTEADS

No single moment sparked Blackdom's revival and Afro-Frontier town. More than likely, the level of Black land ownership and the ability to own a whole square mile of land after 1909 contributed to propel Blackdom forward when racial tensions increased over the course of the first decade of the twentieth century. The Blackdom Townsite Company became increasingly important to keep the vision of Black prosperity alive in the county.

TALLMADGE AFFAIR

The indictment of the Tallmadge brothers during the early period of Blackdom's history may also have played a role in Blackdom's early stunted beginning. The "Tallmadge affair" was a peripheral incident worth mentioning for the sake of inclusion. A national story, the wealthy industrialists had millions of dollars—as well as their sovereignty—to lose. Isaac Jones and the greater Jones family disappeared from public record along with Mack Taylor, who homesteaded adjacent to highway 285 east and directly across from the Jones homestead. Dramatically, violence broke out on the streets of Roswell as the federal government authorities added co-conspirators to the allegations against the Tallmadge brothers. Written about in the region's newspaper of record, the Tallmadge affair was notable for a few reasons. It is also likely that many of the events that occurred had no relation to one another.

The Tallmadge brothers (Chester and Benjamin), railroad tycoons from Chicago, Illinois, made a series of land deals that sparked the attention of authorities, and on June 24, 1905, the *Los Angeles Herald* reported the arrest of the brothers on federal land fraud charges. According to the article, "Revelations expected to fully equal those made in Oregon and Montana."[25] United States Commissioner Karl Snyder required Benjamin Tallmadge to post a $5,000 bond for his appearance. Commissioner Snyder issued a warrant because of the complaint of Interior Department Agent Grosvenor Clarkson (a government investigator). According to charges against the Tallmadge brothers, they procured some of New Mexico's most valuable land with fraudulent homestead entries. "This land, unimproved, sells from $20 to $30 an acre. All these cases are under investigation. Mr. Tallmadge declares that all of his dealings have been according to law and that it will be so proven."[26]

Carl C. Young and John McGintry, business associates of the Tallmadge brothers, were charged with perjury and subornation of perjury in the Tallmadge affair.[27] William Overstreet, another business acquaintance of the Tallmadge brothers, swung on Agent Clarkson after the news of his indictment. The government alleged land fraud and Overstreet claimed Clarkson engaged in extrajudicial persecution.[28] Overstreet beat Clarkson "like he stole something" in front of Main Street's onlookers. In July 1905, the Tallmadge brothers' land fraud cases were dismissed, except for the associated perjury charges, which remained until 1907.[29] Wealthy and well connected, the Tallmadge brothers in August 1907 received a favorable ruling from the Territorial Supreme Court.[30]

In the midst of New Mexico's transition into statehood, Blackdom's ascendance appeared blunted at the beginning. Possibly, Blackdomite leaders feared implication in a regional land fraud case a few months before it was set to open in 1904. The first president and vice president of the Blackdom Townsite Company, Frank Boyer and Isaac Jones may have felt a heavy responsibility as heads of a company. Blackdom Townsite Company wasn't implicated in any known documents; however, land fraud and shell companies were common. Coincidentally, a year after incorporation, Blackdom had no address and appeared in full decline by the summer of 1904.

In addition to a steep learning curve and a lack of full engagement in Blackdom, Chaves County was steeped in legal fights over land that may explain Blackdom's precarious start. Chester and Benjamin Tallmadge were loosely connected to Blackdom in their frontier scheme of buying failed desert homesteads for purposes against federal law. Third-party purchases of homestead land were a violation of federal law. In an example of shifty dealings, Mack Taylor sold a homestead with a warranty deed on April 9, 1904, to Charles Tannehill, a wealthy California businessman living in Roswell.[31] Only a month earlier, Taylor successfully completed his homestead and was granted his patent by the Land Office in Roswell. In June 1905, Tannehill sold the land to the Tallmadge brothers.

CHAPTER 5

AFROTOPIA

READER DISCRETION ADVISED

The current public discourse to emphasize consensual engagement amongst people, including children, requires my acknowledgment of a gendered, masculine, male privilege that handicaps my ability to fully explore the ontology of women, children, and queer folks. The presence of Kahtia, a gendered daughter and teenager in my life, provides an impetus to venture into an unknown private conscious space. At the intersection of Black women, the Borderlands, and a Black masculine male-dominated society, there are no current literary systems to ask permission to peek behind the veil of Black womanhood. Because of my perspective as a "trained" patriarch, all the narrow understandings in this chapter confirm the critiques of a masculine male-dominated society.

Instead of ignoring or engaging in reductionism, the injurious nature of exclusionary as well as binary historical frameworks requires a brief synopsis of where my shortcomings begin. As a child of a poor Black woman living in South Central Los Angeles, I caught glimpses of how dehumanizing a patriarchal society could be for a young (unwed) Black woman. Veretha, my mother, dropped out of Locke High School after birthing me at the age of 15. Veretha was part of a Black migration out of Mississippi, whose father settled on the West Coast after his military service. Unaware of the "dark alliance" that exacerbated traumas in our de-industrialized working-class community (48th and Western), Veretha was poisoned by the patriarchy, and I was sent to live with my grandparents in Compton, California.[1]

The poisoned patriarchy inspired artists who created poems about my mother's cohort of Black women and set it to music. Disrespect turned to disregard as Veretha's body transitioned from a young female body to a middle-aged much deteriorated female body. She was a proud Black woman whose ontology was most vivid to me, as a child, on Sundays. In the back of a triplex next to the alley off 47th, my mom would cook and clean our 900-square-foot pad singing the music of The Dells. Cue the drum roll: "Give your baby a standing ovation."

In the assailable patriarchy of my grandparents' house, my grandmother's power lorded over the private sphere and my grandfather dutifully performed in the public sphere. When Mary Elizabeth Gilmore Nelson (my grandmother) felt her power was insufficient she would say, "Wait 'til daddy gets home." Within our vulnerable patriarchal family, my grandmother's matriarchal power included the ability to add capacity to her enforcement. Moreover, Mary E. Nelson was a matriarch within our church community, which further added to her sphere of influence in our urbanized Black Cowboy society. After bearing eight children and raising them and me, in her 50s she started college. In her 60s, she established a business called Grandma's House, a daycare. In her 70s, her business grew into a school called Trinity Unlimited Outreach - Childcare Center that her daughters and granddaughters now manage. My grandfather, Glenorce, owned and operated a family business (near the beach) with his sons for fifty years; now he helped finance my grandmother's dream.

This two-part chapter was conceived with my observations engaging a Black "cowboy" society expectant to become a patriarch. Through the narrow windows of my mother and grandmother's life, I "saw" a mirror image in the public record of Mattie/Mittie Moore (Wilson) and Ella (McGruder) Boyer. Blackdom entered a period of revival after 1909 because of the omnipresent Black matriarchal power. Blackdomite women were Black women in a Victorian-*ish* society; homesteading was central to Blackdom and women were keenly aware and exploited the opportunity to become public-facing colonizers. Although female in an anemic patriarchal society, women helped double Blackdom's landholdings by 1919.

Lastly, this chapter assumes my need to do more work to better tell the story of Black women in Blackdom. As a male, masculine, man, coming of age in Compton during the 1990s, I am not the best prepared scholar to write a history of Black women in the Borderlands. From behind the border wall of my poisoned patriarchal understanding, I peer into a neighboring moth-eaten matriarchal space to illuminate what was apparent. Dehumanization of Black women during my training as a patriarch was infused with Black ontology in my songs of youth.

Be forewarned: I mimicked a pattern of dehumanization as I floated down the 91 freeway with my dad in his Cadillac (for the year); at audio decibels far higher than was safe for a child, violins began to play, dramatic drum roll, "This is a man's world . . . but it wouldn't be nothing . . . without a woman or a little girl."[2] When I was old enough to drive, I attempted to manifest the ontological space of my father with the new music of the day. My granddad bought me a powder blue 1975 VW bug (fuel injected). I kept my rims clean, with tinted windows and racing tires in the back. One might have seen me floating down Crenshaw; at audio decibels far higher than was safe for a teenager, cue the stripped drum track: "A bitch iz a bitch."[3]

Again, cognizant of the varying degrees of disrespect and dehumanization manufactured in a poisoned patriarchy, my understanding of Black women's ontology began at "dehumanizing" and shifted to dehumanizing. This humble and pedestrian telling of Black women's stories emanates from a limited feminist "knowledge" (and critique).

I have an even more limited set of knowledges (and critique) from the LGBTQIA+/- community perspective. My one or two courses exploring queer theory don't qualify me to carefully and fully engage the ontology of the communities.

Nevertheless, it is impossible to analyze Blackdom's revival and only consider the efforts of "masculine" men. This chapter focuses on the ontology of Black women in a borderland that extended beyond their veiled existence within the White hegemonic society, to the best of my ability. Blackdom was a vulnerable patriarchy in both the public and private spheres of influence, and Black women bore the semi-silent burden.[4] Blackdomite society was a patriarchy that functioned when matriarchs fully accepted the exchange. In Roswell, however, Black women were more often charged for domestic violence than were men. Publicly in Chaves County, misogyny and misandry circulated on the minstrel theater stage and in newspaper articles, particularly in the post–WWI era.

In Blackdom prior to 1919, evidence suggests the space had a symmetrical power system as more women entered the homestead class. In part due to the triad of ministers, military personnel, and Freemasons, Blackdom was an ordered society where Blackdomite women flourished. Gendered and accepting of assailable patriarchal rule, Blackdomite women possessed public as well as private power on land they owned.

BLACKDOMITE WOMEN AND THEIR HISTORY: INTRODUCTION

There was a clear outsized influence of women who motivated, moved, and shifted Blackdomite society using the homestead process as leverage in what was a constant set of private negotiations. As Blackdomite children grew into the homestead class, they articulated the striving of feminine, female, matriarchal Blackdom. Black women's ontology, while a mystery to me, in this chapter engages Blackdom's feminine, female, women's Afro-Frontierism as a signifier of the collective conscience. As indicated in homestead records, one might perceive the "virgin/whore" phenomenon represented in the documented history of Ella Boyer and Mittie Moore.[5] However, in this narrative about Blackdomite womanhood, I deliberately articulate duality in my presentation of Mattie/Mittie Moore. Welcoming more study and critique, we also explore Blackdomite society through documents that do not lend themselves to critique or analysis of Blackdom's children as they engaged Afro-Frontierism.

Blackdomites produced a messianic sovereignty. Recent studies suggest patriarchy embodies the "poison" of Black society during the twentieth century. Thoughtfully, yet blindly, we venture to engage the dynamism of women in Blackdomite society through their public records with Black men in their periphery. The Enlargement Act, signed February 19, 1909, began a new era in Blackdom's homestead-class growth as they positioned themselves to smoothly enter the Roaring Twenties in boom times. In Revival, people who endured harsh dry growing seasons got reprieve and the laws changed to allow for accumulation of thousands of miles of (stolen Indigenous) land. The passage of the Enlargement Act was the first of many new US colonization tactics to encourage homesteader occupation and of confiscated Indigenous desert land in Mexico's northern frontier, and women led the charge. Most importantly, the rains came.

Mattie

Mattie (or Mittie) Moore enters Blackdom's narrative with a town in revival as a land donor. The exchange of land was an effort to officially attach the idea of Blackdom to a federal and local registry of homestead land patents. On Indigenous land, partitioned behind the veil of Blackness and Blackdomite society, Black women were landlords. After 1909, Black women thrust themselves into the homestead class—beyond notions of freedom and "promised land"—to solidify generational sovereignty in Afrotopia. While Blackdomite children grew up and married amongst one another, there was no such rule (written or otherwise) that men were required to carry the public burden of engaging hegemonic society beyond the veil of Blackness or Blackdomite society. In Blackdom, directly and indirectly, Black women lorded over more land than Blackdomite men and were omnipresent in society.

Colonizing "free" government land was formulaic, but often expensive to prove up. While it is clear how Black men rented their labor as they started homesteads, it was unclear how the women of Blackdom organized resources and the capacity to ascend Afrotopia outside of the rural family labor structure. In the case of Mattie of Blackdom, I make the assumption that she was Mittie Moore of Roswell, an infamous bootleg'n, gun-slang'n, homestead'n madame. The selective storytelling saves space for Mittie's ascendancy into Blackdom's elite during the Harlem Renaissance, when matriarchs such as Ella Boyer exited. No present documentation suggests the two women ever spoke, face to face. Evidence suggests, however, that when Blackdom's society shifted to a more extractive model for "Blackdom," Mittie Moore's ownership of a whole square mile south of Blackdom in the fall of 1922 had little to do with Blackdom selling the church by the summer.

Lillian

Lillian Collins, of the influential Blackdomite Collins family who moved to Chaves County in 1908, sat down for an interview with Elvis Fleming from the Southeastern New Mexico Historical Society in 1985. Lillian's interview offered flashes of faded memory. Beyond what appeared in the documented interview, I asked Elvis if he recalled any off-record comments, but too much time had passed to remember.

Lillian recalled her family's move to Roswell and the tremendous hostility they faced when New Mexico was on the eve of statehood. Full Blackdomite manifestation included dual residency: Blackdom (rural) and Roswell (city). Women with children more than likely dictated in which space they lived; it was unlikely that children had much say in the matter. According to Lillian, who was speaking to a White man (and was therefore possibly constrained in her communications), she recalled Black kids attending the local high school and the segregated school system's refusal to grant diplomas. Blackdomite children in Roswell had entered a foreign space hostile to their presence. Hazel Taylor Parker provides a confirmation of Lillian's account of increased racial tension around the same time in Chaves County. "After Dexter [a nearby town] started settling in, well, the people who was comin', they was prejudiced in their hearts. Anyway, they did not want the negroes around and this is why they moved further out."[6]

In 1908, when Lillian first moved as a child with her family, Roswell was a fairly integrated city. Not leaving the impression of a totally hostile society, to Elvis she said, "When we moved to town we did not really have the problem because, uh, they were such sweet people, uh, of any race."[7] Lillian continued, "The Mexicans and Whites were mostly welcoming . . . [but] we had a problem in the latter years when the kids would have rock fights," referring to "Anglo" kids from a different school versus the "Coloreds" from her school. The fight continued until someone called "the law."

THE REVIVAL, PART 1 (1909–1915)

Ella Boyer was an archetypal Blackdomite woman whose life and vocation as a formally trained midwife focused on children. During Ella's tenure engaging the Borderlands, she held office in the Order of the Eastern Star, an auxiliary organization of Black Freemasonry. Ella bore and raised ten children and homesteaded on 160 acres on the eve of boom times. Her power emanated from her relationship with Frank (Freemason, patriarch, and devout husband) as well as her children who carried with them family traditions to places like Southern California. Ella's influence extended beyond the private sphere as she thrust herself into Blackdom's homestead class, leveraging her power as a matriarch.

Blackdomites were not satisfied with a loose unincorporated town, and the 1909 Homestead Enlargement Act became a major catalyst for further development. Black people were inspired by the prospect of maturing the idea of Blackdom as well as their investment in context of

New Mexico's statehood, which further partitioned Mexico's northern frontier. An incorporated all-Black town showed potential for generational wealth creation. Ella Boyer, née McGruder, was one of the first Blackdomite women to homestead and kick-start the Revival.

By 1912, on the eve of New Mexico's incorporation as a state of the union, Blackdom was revived and fully functioning as a thriving unincorporated Afro-Frontier town. During World War I, Blackdomite children were conscripted from "Blackdom" and, therefore, federally recognized. Most important to Blackdom's future economic prospects, oil exploration in the Permian Basin exploded. In May 1920, Black folks (Blackdomites) solidified their place in the region's oil boom, with Black women in the forefront of the Afro-Frontier scheme. Blackdomites maximized opportunity behind the corporate veil of their municipality.

Ella Boyer was a well-educated Black woman from Georgia who literally brought life into Blackdomite society. Trained at the Haines Institute (founded by Miss Lucy Laney), Ella honed her midwifery skills. She "officiated so many births there were too many to count."[8] Traveling by train from Georgia, she joined her husband with a group of children and family large enough to fill up a baseball field. Her 1900 migration and settlement in the New Mexico Territory included ten children by the census of 1910. According to Ella's homestead records, she began a 160-acre homestead north of and adjacent to what would become the forty-acre Blackdom town square.

1909

On February 19, 1909, the US Congress increased the homestead allotment to 320 acres and up to 640 acres or a whole square mile. Theoretically, provided the land was hard to irrigate, if all of Ella Boyer's children owned the maximum amount of homestead land, they would possess the equivalent land mass of present-day Compton, California. In 1910, Blackdom emerged when bitter battles became what was known as the Mexican Revolution. Militarily strategic against Pancho Villa's raids, New Mexico was "on the verge of statehood," and

Blackdomites had positioned themselves to take advantage of the shift from federal territory to state status. Including the era of Blackdom's Roaring Twenties, they indulged in Afrotopia and found exponential growth as the Revival led to boom times.

Consequently, more Blackdomite women joined the homestead class. Opportunistically, Frank Boyer became an assignee for Mattie Moore and Pernecia Russell under the amendment to the homestead laws. Blackdomites were a part of the homesteader boom that by 1910 helped colonize over 40 million acres with a hundred thousand land patents. Blackdom Townsite inspired Black people to homestead until the Great Depression. According to new law, Frank was allowed to file a land patent for Mattie and Pernecia without land counting as part of his maximum allotment. Frank Boyer began a homestead patent for the forty acres for Blackdom's town square devoting Mattie's thirty-five acres and Pernecia's five acres. Along with Ella's 160 acres, the forty acres of Blackdom town square helped solidify the Boyer family's Blackdom legacy.

In 1909, one of New Mexico's first oil wells was drilled in Eddy County, in the Lake Arthur village area, where the Boyer family lived for a while when they were in Blackdom or Dexter. A convergence of positive events combined with Blackdomite boldness and inspired a second major wave of homesteading families. Proving up land continued to be a difficult feat. Ella Boyer got caught up and had to provide a deposition before completion of her almost decadelong homestead process. Desert-land entry homestead patents required one to show significant improvements. On November 22, 1910, Ella Boyer filed the annual paperwork required. She invested $1,237, but there was not sufficient irrigation to satisfy the General Land Office in Roswell. Her process dragged on, requiring that she testify. All homestead patents required legal procedures and federal perjury charges were a consequence for false information on proving up papers.

In 1909, 40-year-old Mattie Moore from Donley County, Texas, made her homestead claim as sole heir of Dickson Garner under the

Soldier's Additional Homestead Right process (with Frank Boyer as assignee).[9] As assignee, Frank was able to take over Moore's homestead patent in the name of Dickson Garner, her supposedly dead soldier husband.[10] The heirs of Dickson Garner already claimed land using those benefits, and Mattie needed a new story. Mattie Moore's homestead entry in 1909 led to the initial investigation and rejection of the paperwork for 34.79 acres of Blackdom's town square.

David Geyer, a lawyer in Roswell, helped Frank in his duties as assignee and was granted the power of attorney.[11] Mattie wrote to Peter Keller, commissioner of the Buffalo, Missouri, General Land Office, with a story about her two sisters who died in infancy. Nothing moved Keller to grant Mattie her claim. Moore then attempted to claim sole heirship of "Dixon" Garner. W. A. Dixon, Chester Q. Dixon, and Margaret White of Conway County, Arkansas, transferred an additional right for eighty acres as the sole heirs of Allen Dixon, who was assumed to go by the alias Dixon Garner/Dickson Garner. In February 1911, the General Land Office in Washington, DC, answered the request of the Roswell General Land officer requesting a ruling on Mattie Moore's claim. On the eve of New Mexico statehood, Blackdomites' forty-acre town square was in limbo.

Mattie Moore, Pernecia Russell, and Ella Boyer faced many obstacles in entering Blackdom's homestead class. Ella, Mattie, and Pernecia applied for homestead patents under the additional lands provision and received tremendous scrutiny. Frank Boyer appealed. Aside from the male-dominated historical record of Blackdom, Mattie Moore, Pernecia Russell, and Ella Boyer were foundational. As assignee of Pernecia Russell, Frank Boyer was in a fight for Blackdom's five acres. After another investigation, the Roswell General Land Office found that the widow of John B. Russell (Pernecia) had already made her claims to an allotment of 45.01 acres years earlier under the assignee Francis F. Bamforth in Wyoming. Pernecia Russell (allegedly) sold land to J. T. Pendleton as well. Thus, Pernecia had exhausted her right to homestead land.[12]

Blackdomite society continued to expand as Blackdom's town square languished. Peter Collins earned his family's first patent in 1909, as the Collins family settled into the dual investment of a home in town (City of Roswell) and a ranch in Blackdom. Monroe and Thomas, Peter's brothers, completed homestead patents in 1914. Peter, not to be outdone, earned his second homestead patent in 1915. Another brother, Frederick, earned his first in 1916. Thomas E. (son of Thomas) completed his first patent as the US engaged in world war. As Blackdom entered boom times in 1919, Thomas senior applied for a second patent, betting his land on the Blackdom Oil Company.

1910 CENSUS

Through a narrow window of refuge, Frank Boyer succeeded by the time of the taking of the 1910 US census in Chaves County, New Mexico. However, Blackdom made his achievement as the first president of the state's only platted and incorporated "exclusive Negro settlement" significant. The Santa Fe Pacific Railroad Company was interested in acquiring one million five hundred thousand acres in the Pecos Valley Region and guaranteed land in an all-Black town a worthy investment.[13] Chaves County had a population of 17,000 while Eddy had 12,000 residents. There were 233 Black people in Roswell and fifty-six in Artesia circa 1910.

> "Blackdom Wants a School": *Santa Fe New Mexican*, October 13, 1910 Exclusive Negro Settlement | Superintendent of Public Instruction James E. Clark today had a letter from Blackdom, twenty miles south of Roswell and near Dexter, Chaves County, asking for advice as to school curriculum. The letter states that Blackdom is the only exclusive negro settlement in New Mexico, that the colored people have taken up 10,000 acres in homesteads and will install a pumping plant. The community has built a commodious school house and now asks for assistance in arranging for the curriculum and a teacher.

1911 "NEGRO THANKSGIVING"

Blackdom bustled by 1911, and the Boyer family decisions dictated the direction of the Black municipality. Racialization pressures in the region incentivized the Blackdomite revival.

In an interview with Maisha Baton, Roosevelt Boyer Sr. (Frank Boyer's son, born January 26, 1906) claimed that Frank Boyer would have been rich if he could harness the power "he got his hands on"—referring to the Blackdom Townsite Company. Intimately familiar with the pervasive White consciousness in the region, Frank Boyer believed that those who embodied hegemonic society would "make it [living/homesteading] cost more for negroes." Roosevelt recalled how emphatic his father was about not building Blackdom when he said, "I don't want to do it. I won't do it." Frank Boyer and his cohort of Blackdomites persisted by teaching sovereignty in church and Masonic meetings. They decided to reimagine Blackdom.

Blackdom's rebranding began in February 1911, when the General Land Office in Washington, DC, answered the Roswell General Land officer request for a ruling on Mattie Moore's claim. Hoping to plat and announce the address of Blackdom, Blackdomites were faced with testimony of the commissioner of the Buffalo, Missouri, General Land Office Peter Keller. In short, Blackdom's land patent was rejected; there were inconsistencies in Mattie's story. Heirs of Allen Dixon had received land allotments as Dixon Garner, spawning further investigation.[14]

Black people in diaspora united at the intersection of a similar consciousness established a physical location signifying God's sovereignty: Blackdom. At a time of great progress and celebration, on December 7, 1911, Artesia's *Pecos Valley News* reported on a "Negro Thanksgiving":

> The Blackdom population has imbibed the spirit of the valley times and have organized a Boosters' club. This club gave a banquet Thanksgiving evening. Blackdom is the negro town of the Pecos Valley, eighteen miles east of Roswell. Its citizenship and officials are composed entirely of the colored people. Francis Boyer was the

> toastmaster of the evening. Toasts were responded to by the following gentlemen:
>
> "Immigration," W. M. Young. "Our School, "James Eubank. "What we produce," Daniel G. Keys. Music. "Real Estate," W. M. Young. "Pumping and Windmills," Clinton Ragsdale. "Possibilities in Livestock," George Wilson. Music. "Business opportunities," G. W. Wilson. Music. "Homesteading," Monroe Collins. Songs to enliven the occasion were sung by the Dixie Chorus and the best instrumental music attainable was on hand. The menu was made up of the products of Blackdom.[15]

There was no official start to the revival, but if there was an inauguration of the new era, Blackdom's 1911 Thanksgiving served as that moment. On January 6, 1912, the Afro-Frontier town had developed into an ordered society in time for New Mexico to become the forty-seventh state. After a year of *mitote* about New Mexico's statehood, Blackdomite hope was reflected in their rebranding.

On December 30, the *Santa Fe New Mexican* reported, "Blackdom Amends Charter: Colony of Negroes Found a Townsite in Chaves County."[16] Designated Secretary of the Blackdom Townsite Company Wesley T. Williams partnered with Frank, who remained president, and Ella Boyer became vice president.[17] A few days earlier, Wesley became the first Black man appointed to the position of United States Commissioner in New Mexico. According to the article, "The Blackdom Townsite Company of Blackdom, Chaves County, today filed amendments to their charter with Nathan Jaffa, secretary of the territory. The amendments concern a change in the number of directors allowed the company. Blackdom is a colony of negroes." Blackdom's future was secured by the three officers.

A surge of Black people in Chaves County joined Blackdom's homestead class, and the phenomenon continued for two decades. Longtime supporters of Blackdom such as Charley Thompson began homesteads after years of little motivation. Charley's wife Emma moved to the homestead, and they completed the process on January 23, 1914. Wesley Williams finalized his first homestead on October 15, 1914. The Thompson family was typical of the converted Blackdomites who bought into the Afro-Frontier scheme in the context of New Mexico's statehood and Blackdom's Revival. After Charley signed the articles of incorporation in 1903, he worked as a janitor in Roswell during the lost years (1903–1911). The town of Blackdom in Revival reestablished Charley and the Thompson family in regional markets as they ascended into Afrotopia.

1912 LUCY HENDERSON

Two days prior to statehood, William C. Henderson completed his first homestead in the New Mexico Territory. The new buzz about Blackdom began when the *Chicago Defender* published Lucy Henderson's letter that proclaimed Blackdomites' ascendance into Afrotopia. Founded in 1905, the Black newspaper was a major outlet to Black thinkers and doers. Lucy's letter expressed the freedom of Chaves County and the sovereignty of Blackdom.[18] She was amazed at the amount of "free land."

Lucy didn't appear on record as homesteading; however, on February 13, 1911, George W. Henderson, in partnership with his brothers Ash and Marshall, homesteaded 320 acres in the State of New Mexico. Edward F. Henderson (George's brother) completed his forty-acre homestead in March. Curiously, the Henderson group of homesteads extended beyond the borders of Blackdom and mimicked the creation of a separate Afro-Frontier town and forty-acre town square. In the absence of new evidence, one assumes the Henderson family helped organize a sister community south of Blackdom near Artesia with their combined 640 acres (whole square mile). On the eve of Blackdom's boom time, George E. Henderson desired a stake in Blackdom Oil and completed a homestead in Blackdom's commons on August 12, 1918.

At a time of tremendous violence against people under the conditions of "Americanism," Lucy's letter signified security compared to the exploited and indebted rural classes of Black folks at the time. A cohort of Black women entered leadership roles in Blackdom, particularly after April 10, 1912, when the town got a post office, which Bessie E. Malone managed for years and into the WWI period.

In December 1912, James Harold Coleman placed an advertisement in *The Freeman* (Indianapolis, Indiana) that read, "WANTED 500 Negro families (farmers preferred) to settle on FREE Government Lands in Chaves County, New Mexico. Blackdom is a Negro colony. Fertile soil, ideal climate. No 'Jim Crow' Laws. For more information write James Harold Colman." The headline, "WANTED," was larger than the article. James was drawn to Blackdom for many reasons after divorce from his first wife, Julia Pearl.

Significantly, James Coleman nurtured his relationships in the Black literary network of people, institutions, and outlets when he resettled in Blackdom. Anti-lynching was the focal point of Black activist media campaigns at the time, and the Blackdom phenomenon became a salvific experiment for Black folks catching hell in neighboring states. James, one of Black America's "Who's Who," was associated with "In Interesting Race News" (*Topeka Plaindealer*), December 20, 1912. "Colored people have established a town called Blackdom in New Mexico near the line. It is made up by people from Georgia, Tennessee, Kentucky, Illinois, California, Texas and Virginia." Further skimming revealed, "At Mounds Bayou, Miss., Negroes own and operate a $100,000 oil mill," touting the greatness of independently wealthy Black people who settled in all-Black towns in the South with Jim Crow. For the more enterprising, "Frank Brown, a young colored man of Baltimore, Md, who has an invention designed for the elimination of the use of coal and to reduce the cost of labor. It is called a wave and gravity motor." James Coleman was the conduit for Blackdom's rebranding during Revival.

1913 *THE CRISIS* MAGAZINE

Julia Pearl Hughes (Coleman-Robinson) was born to John and Mary Hughes in Melville Township, Alamance County, North Carolina, and was the first African American woman to successfully own and operate her own drugstore. Julia graduated in 1893 from Scotia Seminary (now Barber–Scotia College) in Concord, North Carolina, and in1897 graduated from the Pharmaceutical College at Howard University. She relocated to Philadelphia, Pennsylvania, to do postgraduate work at the Philadelphia College of Pharmacy and managed the Frederick Douglass Hospital pharmacy. In 1899, Dr. Hughes opened her own drugstore, Hughes Pharmacy, at 937 Christian Street in South Philadelphia.

On February 16, 1900, Dr. Hughes married James Harold Coleman, a traveling journalist from Virginia. Julia and James moved to Newport News, Virginia, and Dr. Coleman opened a pharmacy. Successful for over a decade, they started the Columbia Chemical Company in 1909. The Coleman partnership created the hair-care product Hair-Vim, but they dissolved the business after a year and headed towards divorce. In 1912, James Coleman accepted the Chaves County challenge and relocated. Julia moved to Washington, DC, to stay with her relatives. In 1914, Julia started a weekly newspaper with Timothy Thomas Fortune, called the *Weekly Sun*. She rebranded and established the Hair Care-Vim Chemical Company in the basement of her family's home and was officially divorced from James, in 1916, with no children. From January through December, the Blackdom advertisement maintained James Coleman's signature cartoonish use of "WANTED," with the type font size equal to the size of the rest of the words.

1914 ANITA SCOTT COLEMAN

Blackdom was a transcolonial, transnational, and transitional space contextualized by the US–Mexico Borderlands. The NAACP contacted Blackdomites to serve as a temporary refuge to help Marie Scott's brother escape to Mexico. Marie, a 17-year-old Black girl, was raped by two drunken White men who "skulked into the black residential section of Wagoner, Oklahoma, looking for female sexual prey." Marie's brother heard her cry, came to her rescue, and killed Lemuel Pease, one of the attackers. Both the sister and brother fled, but the sister was hunted, caught, and jailed; a mob overran the jail and hanged her on March 31, 1914.

James Coleman answered the NAACP's request for Blackdomite help to provide refuge to the fugitive. James advertised Blackdom in *The Crisis* for a second year throughout 1914 with his name as the official contact. Marie Scott's brother reportedly told the porters that he murdered Pease when he found the men trying to rape Marie.[19] Through a network of Afro-Frontierist communities, Blackdom served public and private means when the space became a stop on the way to Mexico.

In 1916, James married again to Anita Scott in Blackdom, from where they engaged the New York literary community. The marriage of the Colemans, Black folks inspired by Blackdom's revival, mimicked the time of renewal and rebirth. Anita and James of Blackdom had two children. Anita Coleman was born in Mexico where her Buffalo Soldier father retired in Sonora, Mexico, around 1890. During the Harlem Renaissance she, like James, appeared in the pages of *The Crisis* magazine. Anita Scott Coleman's work has been posthumously published under the title "Unfinished Masterpiece."[20] Consistent during the Harlem Renaissance, those who had the means escaped rural life for the big city. James got a job in Los Angeles, and they left Blackdom before the "Great crash."

THE REVIVAL, PART 2 (1917–1919)

On November 1, 1917, the *Roswell Daily Record* reported "Guilt Not Proven":

> Not proven was the result of the city against Mittie Moore in Judge Parsons' court this afternoon. As evidence of what City Attorney John E. Clayton and the police force is up against this case is a good example. Sunday night at the home of Mittie Moore, a dive on South Virginia, two pistol shots were fired. This morning the city attorney and chief of police visited Hampton Lee, a negro in the employ of the Elks Saloon. Lee stated that Mittie had fired two shots at one John

> Wilson, that both shots passed through Wilson's coat and that he stood by and watched Wilson take the gun away from Mittie. This afternoon when placed on the witness stand, he denied all these facts, saying that he was blocks away when the shooting occurred. So it is that Mittie is free again.[21]

1915 MITTIE'S 640 ACRES THREE MILES SOUTH OF BLACKDOM TOWN SQUARE

Mittie (Mattie) Moore was a Black woman who embodied Chaves County's vice-driven economies through the Great Depression, which brought death to the old Blackdomite society. Unashamed, Mittie was unapologetic and helped further embolden people like Dixie Porter. In the spring of 1917, America entered World War I and the conscripted children in Chaves County appeared on the front page (above the fold) of the *Roswell Daily Record*. Editors at the newspaper felt it important to also print a story about Dixie Porter's problems with the law. Perhaps as noteworthy as the list of conscripts in Chaves County, Dixie was the aggressor in a domestic violence case against her husband. Dixie's public utterances as well as her ties to Mittie feature in a veiled reference to "South Virginia Ave."

Mittie Moore had many encounters with Roswellian authorities. Beginning in 1914, her body became a subject of Roswell's legal system. In Revival, Blackdomites were more discerning, and Mittie's activities were the antithesis of their intellectual, religious, and agricultural society. Neither Roswell nor Blackdom were spaces that appreciated Mittie's presence. Chaves County was open to prostitution. For example, Pauline Garnett was found guilty of the offense without any fanfare on October 8, 1912. The city fined Pauline $25, and she immediately paid it in full. Edith Garnett was also arrested October 8, on the charge of "being a bawdy house inmate." The city fined Edith $25 and she promptly paid her fees in full.

In 1913, the Attorney General of the United States began selecting local "white-slave officers" in the newly created states of Arizona, Texas, and New Mexico.[22] As a result, New Mexican legislators marginalized "houses of ill repute" throughout the state. By March 1914, the city of Roswell adopted Ordinance 33 of Section 64, making prostitution a misdemeanor subject to fines and thirty days in jail plus the original fine that came along with being caught engaging in bawdy business. Being an "inmate" in a bawdyhouse was an offense against a city ordinance that was expanded to curtail the activities that led to Mittie's takeover of the city's vice in 1913. In 1914, Mittie Moore was arrested for prostitution. It was during this period when Mattie exited public records and Mittie entered public records.

In June 1914, Mattie Moore's assignee Frank Boyer triumphed in getting the land dispute case reopened. Mattie vanished from public record, but Mittie appeared. During the same month, the city of Roswell charged Carman Kyle with "violating Section 64 Ordinance 33, being an inmate of a bawdy house." Carman was found guilty, fined $25, and immediately paid the fine in full.[23] The city of Roswell charged Mittie for violating section 62 of Ordinance 33 of the Compiled Ordinances of the city of Roswell—setting up and keeping a house of assignation and prostitution—changing the relationship between the Black bawdy business she operated and the city.[24] Mittie was fined $50, double the price to be paid and thus a de facto Jim Crow style of law enforcement.

Mittie challenged the discretion of Peace Officer Kirby, who was the arresting officer. Mittie appealed the case and requested a jury trial, a platform that couldn't be denied her. Mittie defended herself with the medieval legal strategy, Contempt of the Sovereign, in the case of *City of Roswell v. Richardson*.[25] Statehood made the legal strategy obsolete because the sovereignty of individuals in the territory transferred to the "sovereign" State of New Mexico. Mittie's case ascended to the newly established state Supreme Court in Santa Fe.

In the area, Blackdomites employed the expertise of attorney George Malone who was the first Black man to try a case in front of New Mexico's state Supreme Court. In 1915, Mittie's appeal of her conviction led to the New Mexico Supreme Court. Mittie's action pitted District Judge Granville A. Richardson against the city of Roswell, against whom he had issued a writ of prohibition.[26] Who had control over Mittie Moore's body was at the core of the debate in this case of jurisdiction. Instead of shrinking her profile and accepting the relationship that Roswell authorities offered to her, she decided against such a precedent. In the end, the petition was dismissed and the alternative writ quashed, upholding the lower court's ruling. Nevertheless, Mittie established herself as a force.

Concurrently, Mittie was becoming a large landowner connected to Blackdom, as she entered a homestead patent under the name Mittie Moore. During the World War I era, Mittie eventually married, becoming Mittie Moore Wilson. She was comfortable in the Roswell sex worker economy, which had become a Chaves County institution. It helped support local government with fines and court fees essentially functioning as taxes but also helped Blackdom, for it was the undergird of the town's relevance through Mittie and her ownership of one square mile.[27] Her relatively routine life became increasingly difficult when city officials used the new conditions created by World War I to curtail Mittie's activities. As the United States entered World War I, Mittie's defiance began representing more than illegality. She became the antithesis of patriotism and the idea of the "citizen soldier."

There was a large investment in the development of an oil industry at the Blackdom Townsite, and the local newspapers began attacking the project by making Mittie the focus.

Public notices were printed in the Roswell newspaper under the heading "Notice for Publication," which was a document that came from the Department of the Interior reporting ownership of land. In the case of Mittie, the US Land Office at Roswell, New Mexico, printed her notice in the newspaper. The notice for Mittie read,

> NOTICE is hereby given that Mittie Moore Wilson, formerly Mittie Moore, of Blackdom, N.M., who, on July 21st, 1915, made

> Homestead entry, No 032454, for W1/2 Section 17, Township 14-S., Range 24-E., N.M.P. Meridian, has filed notice of intention to make three year Proof, to establish claim to the land above described, before Register or Receiver, at U.S. Land Office, Roswell, N.M., on the 14th day of October, 1919.

1916 GEORGE MALONE

Even though the racialization process for Black people was increasingly hostile, New Mexico was still a less threatening place for migration than other racialized spaces. Black men like George Malone moved to New Mexico; he made his way to Blackdom after the 1911–1913 Blackdom advertising campaign. Malone was a lawyer from the South, having graduated from the Central Law School of Walden University, a Black institution in Nashville, Tennessee.

After practicing in Mississippi, he moved to Blackdom in 1914. He was one of the teachers in the town. Malone applied to the New Mexico Supreme Court for a permanent license to practice law.[28] Roswell lawyer Harold Hurd vouched for Malone's integrity and informed the clerk of court "that most of the colored population called upon him for assistance." In early August 1916, the *Rio Grande Republican* announced that Malone was admitted to the state bar, and he "is a negro, and at present the only negro lawyer in New Mexico."[29] Malone became the first Black man to argue in front of the New Mexico Supreme Court in August 1916. Shortly after Malone had his Supreme Court appearance, he moved to Albuquerque to practice law and died within the year.

Because of the inactivity in the town post-1916, many scholars understood the drought of 1916–1917 as the beginning of Blackdom's demise, in part as evidence of the Afro-Frontier town in full decline; however, the activity during that period was misunderstood. Building Blackdom was a business decision instead of a decision to seek refuge. When greater opportunities existed outside of Blackdom, residents of the town prioritized opportunity above all else. While drought destroyed Black wealth in the county at different points in the town's history, Roswell, for example, welcomed Black people as servants. In this scenario, this group of Afro-Frontierists established a dual existence living, working, and communing in White-dominated societies while also maintaining a virtual existence in Blackdom that sometimes materialized in economic and community progress. The real and palpable problems in Frank Boyer's life aside from a 1916 drought supposedly began Blackdom's mass abandonment.[30] Drought conditions did not return until after 1916. Rainfall was 16.82 inches in 1916, 6.21 inches in 1917, and 9.18 inches in 1918.

1917 WORLD WAR I

Eustace Boyer (Frank Boyer's second oldest son) was 24, single, and recently discharged from the US Army. Eustace eventually earned a homestead patent but was part of a cohort of Blackdomite male children conscripted to fight in World War I. Eustace was absent from his homestead starting in October 1917 and ending in April 1919. He started the patent process in December 1916, a year before he volunteered for conscription. Upon his return to Chaves County, he built a one-room box house (12 feet by 14 feet) and one-and-a-half miles of fence and cultivated ten acres, all of which cost about $500.[31]

The Blackdom vision continued into the 1920s. Whole families found opportunity in owning drought-ridden desert lands attached to the idea of Blackdom. At the age of fifty-eight, Erastus Herron and his 52-year-old wife Charlene began their homestead patent process in 1917. The Herron family migrated from South Carolina and supported Blackdom's revival. Queen Ester Herron was the first of the South Carolinian family to homestead in 1914, receiving her patent in 1917. By the 1930s, the Ragsdale family homesteaded close to three square miles in Chaves County, all of which was associated with Blackdom: Clinton (1913, 1920, and 1926), Ezell (1917, and 1921).

CLEANLINESS

In early 1917, the United States prepared to enter World War I, and it did so on April 6. The US government began a propaganda campaign promoting an effort on the home front of the "war" against waste, gluttony, and other unpatriotic behavior. The war effort was both an advantage and a disadvantage to Mittie Moore's business interests. The war economy brought men and money to the area in part because of the New Mexico Military Institute (NMMI) in Roswell. Notions of patriotism and purity were propagated to build up a citizenry to support war. The US government distributed pamphlets that were then printed in local newspapers urging people to do what they could to help.

For people under the conditions of American Blackness, vagrancy laws were used to harass. A key element in the enforcement of White supremacy in the South, the use of vagrancy increased after 1917 in Roswell—a Southern-styled oasis. Specifically, in the case of Mittie Moore, prostitution and vice went from "necessary evil" to an abomination in civil society.

Mittie Moore Wilson married in 1917 and increased her efforts to homestead on desert land. Roswell and the NMMI mobilized for World War I, and Blackdom's growth as a town suffered as the war effort took precedence. Most important, the regional war economy was a reprieve from the persistent droughts that began to worsen throughout the region. Many scholars have argued that the 1916 start of a series of droughts was the cause of Blackdom's decline. However, Blackdomite land holding ballooned through the WWI era and continued into the 1920s. Perhaps droughts pushed Black homesteaders into the city looking for work. Homestead records suggest that short-term abandoning of homesteads was typical over the course of proving up. With the drought began a resultant push of Blackdomites into nearby towns and cities.

An article in the *Roswell Daily Record* noted, in a reference to citizens' contribution to the war effort, that "keeping or setting up of houses of ill fame, brothels, or bawdy houses within five miles of any military camp is prohibited."[32] This idea maintained that "all these provisions and restrictions are in the interest of every right-minded soldier. They go a long way toward insuring clean and healthful living conditions in the camps." Mittie's bawdy district was two miles away from NMMI. Being clean or sanitary was an act of patriotic duty, and being a Black bawdy woman in the bawdy district was considered to be the opposite of patriotic in the above context.

During World War I in the US–Mexico Borderlands, social standardization under the guise of patriotism divided society into citizen and noncitizen, clean and unclean. Eventually, Roswell devolved into a Black and White society as the popular media increased the dehumanization of dark-skinned peoples. Cleanliness, then, operated euphemistically.[33] On February 7, 1917, the *Roswell Daily Record* reported: "The city physician, the chairman of the sanitary committee and the city manager A. G. Jaffa reported that the city was in a most unsanitary condition and should have a general cleanup at once."[34] The politically vulnerable mayor of Roswell, John Mullis, promised to clean up the city as part of his political platform. Mayor Mullis quickly responded to the city manager's declaration and decreed February 12–17 "Sanitary Week." Cleanliness had many meanings, and in the beginning, Mayor Mullis focused on garbage and debris. The City Fathers (city administrators) were in dispute over what to do about the lack of cleanliness in the business district.

Mayor Mullis appointed V. C. Bullard as special watchman; the latter was to respond only to issues pertaining to the business district. The businessmen had to pay Bullard's salary, and he would have all the powers of a police officer. Inspections began on Monday, February 19, to make sure that all debris and garbage was hauled away. City officials were serious about "cleaning up" and declared that all premises found unsanitary would result in an arrest. In the end, Mayor Mullis was able to declare the business district clean, without any arrests having been made.

After the successful trash and debris cleanup campaign, Mayor Mullis shifted his focus to sanitizing Roswell's social blights. The war effort and the patriot purity propaganda campaign motivated efforts to end gambling, excess drinking, and prostitution, among other vices. On March 2, 1917, "a stranger [J. E. Sessions] appeared before Mayor Mullis and complained that he had been robbed of $26 and some change by a woman at the Grand Central Hotel on the corner of [Alameda and Main, half a block from the South Virginia and Alameda intersection]."[35] The new focus of Mullis's cleanup campaign resulted in the conviction of the manager at the hotel for permitting and allowing prostitutes and "lewd women" as guests of the hotel. Mamie Roberts, the manager, was charged with the crime of keeping a bawdyhouse along with Muraie [*sic*] Smith.[36] She was fined $31 ($25 fine and $6 in new fees). The women were also given two options: sixty days in the county jail with a suspended sentence, or removal from the county within forty-eight hours.[37]

According to the Roswell newspaper report, "Mayor Mullis and Night Policeman James W. Johnson [were] doing all possible to break up this kind of business."[38] What followed Mamie Roberts' arrest was an onslaught of raids on all that was "lewd" in the city, specifically that which took place on or near South Virginia Street. Night police officer Jim Johnson targeted Mittie's South Virginia Avenue bawdy district near Alameda on Saturday afternoon, April 1, 1917. Officer Johnson rounded up seven "Negro" women. Each of them pleaded not guilty and were given a trial. After all the evidence was presented to Judge Parsons, they were found guilty and sentenced to a fine of $25 plus $5 dollars in court fees with a thirty-day jail sentence that was ultimately dismissed. Mittie was the target of Mayor Mullis's dragnet, but she eluded the initial assault against her until the mayor finally caught her on April 4, 1917. On April 5, 1917, the *Roswell Daily Record* reported, "Mittie Moore Captured."[39]

Mayor Mullis received great praise for his actions. The local newspaper lauded Mullis's "long strides in the right direction, and many other offenders are at present treading on rather slippery ground and unless either right their ways or depart from these parts forever will one day find themselves before the bar of judgment and the judgment is to be no joke either on their efforts to 'clean-up.'"[40] The other women captured in the sting operation were Lucile Williams, Rebecca Glen, and Ida Watson.[41] Mayor Mullis and night policeman Jim Johnson had many successes in their effort to clean up South Virginia Avenue, and the attack jeopardized Mittie's business.

Targeted, captured, and fined $50, Mittie appeared finally brought to justice. For years, the authorities as well as the public had watched as Mittie operated with virtual immunity, and for a moment, she seemed caught. However, Mittie appealed her case that went to district court and was awarded a dismissal.[42] Increased law enforcement ensnared the women around Mittie as well. Aside from being arrested in the 1917 dragnet in March, on August 9, 1917, a few days after being convicted for beating her husband, the *Roswell Daily Record* reported that "Dixie Porter was released" on a $200 bond. Dixie was charged with larceny for stealing $89 in gold. The targeting of Mittie by social and political elites in the city of Roswell destroyed any possibility of a cordial relationship between the city and Black sex workers. Mittie projected boldness that inspired the women around her.

In August 1917, the War Department sent to local municipalities citizen-soldier handbooks with excerpts printed in newspapers around the country, including the *Roswell Daily Record*.[43] The provisions provided guidelines for a good citizen-soldier, prefaced with the disclaimer, "It is informal in tone and does not attempt to give binding rules and directions."[44] Roswell city officials did not go to the extreme of abiding by the provisions, "Congress has provided that it shall be unlawful to sell any intoxicating liquor including beer, ale, or wine to any officer or member of the military forces while in uniform, an exception being made in a case of liquor required for medical purposes."[45] The handbook was not law but rather suggestive of the kinds of actions delineating patriot from enemy.

One of the major unifying elements for White people in the name of patriotism was brought to bear with the highly publicized D. W.

Griffith film *The Birth of a Nation*.[46] Within the film, there were lines separating good and evil, sanitary and unsanitary, and Black and White. The authoritarian position of a new motion picture technology drew these lines, solidifying boundaries between White and Black as well as patriot from Black. *The Birth of a Nation* was new technology in the racialization process of Black people in Roswell. Blackface minstrelsy was a delivery system of Victorian ideals: White/good/civilized/patriotic versus Black/bad/savage/enemy. With great fanfare, on October 5, 1917, the *Roswell Daily Record* announced that the "master creation" was coming to Roswell for the first time on the 17th, 18th, and 19th of the month.[47]

The plethora of articles about Black deviance, not only in Roswell but around the world, took the anti-Black deviance cleanup campaign to its apogee. On August 4, 1917, on the front page of the *Roswell Daily Record* was the story of Dixie, "a colored lady of South Virginia [who] entered a plea of guilty this morning before Judge Parsons to the charge of using angry words and a few directed blows upon, towards and against the body of her husband, Bruce."[48] Judge Parsons requested that Dixie explain her actions to the court. Her demeanor and all the evidence showed her as the aggressor. Unapologetically, Dixie said that she was "convinced" that Bruce "needed a whipping" and so she gave him one. The city fined Dixie $5. Bruce Porter was charged for fighting with his wife, but the charges were dropped when the court recognized that he was only defending himself.

Mittie owned a few speakeasies in Roswell, and while she was in the Elks Saloon on a Sunday night, she was confronted by her fiancé, James Wilson. With her revolver, Mittie Moore "of South Virginia Avenue" shot at James Wilson twice. She reportedly missed him by only inches, putting two holes in his jacket. This incident was significant enough that the city attorney and chief of police visited Hampton Lee, a Black man who worked at the bar, to find out the whole story. Lee's version of events established that Mittie shot in the direction of James Wilson, who began to wrestle with her and ended the altercation.

Mittie was caught again, it appeared. But when the trial came up and James Wilson was on the witness stand, "he denied all these facts, saying that he was blocks away when the shooting uccurred [*sic*]. So it is that Mittie is free again."[49] Some combination of fear and loyalty prevented James from testifying against Mittie. While building her empire, Mittie embodied the antithesis of Victorian sensibilities, and it set the standard for her workers. On December 5, 1917, the *Roswell Daily Record* featured two stories about Mittie. The first reported the arrest of Novice Eubank, of the Blackdom Eubanks, caught by Officer Jim Johnson in the "home with famous Mittie Moore Wilson on South Virginia."[50]

The headline of the second December 5 piece read, "Mittie Moore Here Again."[51] The article expressed a level of disdain and vitriol that existed for her:

> The police force raided the home of Mittie Moore on South Virginia last night and this morning made charges in Judge Parsons' court against Mittie for running a baudy [*sic*] house. The police say that they have the goods on her this time and for a time at least they will have her placed where the dogs can not bite her.

According to the Police Judge's Docket, CHRONOLOGY Defendant in arraignment, pleads not guilty.

> After hearing the testimony of witness and argument of counsel, the court fines the defendant, Mittie Moore Wilson guilty as charged, and sentences her to fray the costs of this suit and be imprisoned in the City-Jail, at hard labor for a term of thirty days. Defendant being aggrieved at the decision of the court also for and obtains an appeal, upon the presentation and approved of a Bond in the sum of $250. Bond made with R. D. Bill and Frank M. Daniel as sure ties; bond approved and filed with the clerk of the Dist. Court this 24th day of Dec. 1917.[52]

Mittie posted bail and continued to fight. She and Novice Eubank were awarded a not guilty verdict on January 22, 1918, in the appellate court.[53]

The "capture" of Mittie was the end of an era, as the stories about her and the "Black menace" declined dramatically after 1917. Curiously, the *Roswell Daily Record* was obsessed with printing stories about a Black population that numbered less than one percent of the total population in the city. The constant bombardment of stories was an assault on the Black image, which helped in the dehumanization of the infinitesimal Black population.

Part of solidifying the dehumanized image of Black people was the appearance of confirmation of Black people reported as minstrel-like. For example, in April 1917, the *Roswell Daily Record* led the news with the headline, "Negro Shoots—Misses" in an almost cartoonish report of a skirmish between two Black men.[54] According to the article, George Robinson, "a noted negro in celebrity who was arrested for gambling this week, one Will Perkins was a bad shot, who is just out of jail after being convicted of gambling would now be dead."[55] Policeman Jim Johnson was just in time at 106 East Alameda—a block away from the intersection with South Virginia Avenue—outside of the Grand Hotel. Both men had guns and were charged with assault with a deadly weapon. The minstrelsy caricaturing of Black men as comedic, fumbling, awkward, childlike deviants purposely resembled the caricatured version of Black men projected on the pages of the local newspaper and in local theaters.

1918 THOMAS COLLINS

Thomas Collins, a member of the prominent and influential Collins family, was fifty-two when he completed his first homestead patent with the help of homestead proof witnesses William Proffit, George Washington, Nick Gates, and Clinton Ragsdale—all of whom were residents of Blackdom.[56] Thomas had a child and a wife; he could hardly afford a long homestead process. The first year he was able to cultivate about twelve acres of maize and kaffir corn, as he did the second and third year.

Thomas's 1913 crop, on twenty-three acres, included beans; this was his best crop ever. He built a two-room house with a shed for his two horses and a chicken coop and fenced thirty acres of his land with three- and four-string barbed wire. He did everything he could to improve the land.

The Ragsdale family homesteaded close to three square miles in Chaves County in a cluster west of Blackdom over the course of two decades. In 1913, amidst Blackdom's Revival, Clinton Ragsdale completed his first homestead. Clinton's brother, Ezell completed his first in 1917 while preparing for deployment overseas in WWI. Clinton completed his second homestead in 1920, shortly after Blackdomites announced the incorporation of Blackdom Oil. Ezell returned from military service and completed his second homestead in 1921. Clinton completed his third homestead claim in 1926 as a tangible means of his expression of Afrotopia during the Harlem Renaissance.

When Thomas Collins entered his final homestead proof on June 7, 1918, he did not cultivate anything because of severe droughts. Thomas invested and sacrificed for nine years, according to his final homestead proof. Although he endured adverse elements, he was not abandoning Blackdom, and neither did the vast majority. Blackdom residents repeated the tradition of working in the greater Chaves County economy until conditions were such that they were able to refocus on their homesteads and Blackdom.

Erastus Herron was a laborer all his life and traded work for room and board as did many Blacks who migrated to Chaves County with only their labor to offer. Erastus began his homestead process in 1913 living on the Eubank homestead, two miles west of the homestead he finally colonized by May 1914.[57] He made a homestead entry in January 1914. He submitted his final entry in September 1918. However, he faced problems with his application because Clabon Stephens of Blackdom filed an application to contest the entry, claiming that Herron had not established residence on the land. Stephens demanded the rights to the land once the case was over, and an investigation ensued. Curiously, the land was not lush with green pastures or flush with water access. Instead, it was nonmineral and agricultural, chiefly valuable for grazing. All the land was flat and mostly filled with small gravel and stones.

The 1919 investigation revealed that Herron established residence on February 11, 1915, with his family. Before that time, he continued to build when he could. Herron's cultivation of the land consisted of plowing and planting a patch of land four hundred ten feet by two hundred fifty feet in the 1914 season. The house he built was a two-room frame about sixteen feet by twenty-four feet. Aside from the storm house and cellar, there was also a two-wire fence surrounding a field nine hundred feet by twelve hundred feet with an enclosure of three hundred feet by four hundred feet that had a three-wire fence surrounding it.

Bostick, from Roswell, furnished the wire and post under a bartering agreement. Herron was assured that the grazing on his land was temporary and once the agreed upon time was over, Bostick's fence would then be the property of Herron. During the year of the investigation in 1919, Herron faced tremendous odds. He had one milk cow that grazed the land. His daughter had two horses, but the family's two mules died months before the investigation. The land could have been plowed with new mules, but the drought rendered Herron helpless. Raising livestock was the only way to make a profit at the time. Even though there was no known water source for this homestead, Clabon Stephens wanted to take the land for himself under a process of reclamation under the desert land law. Apparently, out of spite, Stephens had a fight with Herron's son and tried to get even with him by interrupting the homestead process.

Nick Gates was a witness on Herron's final proof and was questioned in the investigation on February 8, 1919. Special agent Mason Leming interviewed Gates on his homestead less than a mile away from Herron. Gates stood by his contention that he witnessed Herron cultivate twelve acres. When the questioning intensified, Herron made the statement that the judge got "tangled up," or did not quite understand what he was saying. Gates did attest to the fact that he saw the Herron homestead at least once a week for years. George Malone was postmaster at Blackdom in 1919 when he was interviewed in the case of Erastus Herron. The interview took place at the post office at the Blackdom Townsite. Malone stated that Herron lived on his homestead for at least nine years. Malone, who came to Blackdom in September 1915, lived half a mile from Herron with his family. From 1915 to the time of the investigation, Malone stated, what he witnessed was continuous residence on the part of the Herron family. Malone was not only postmaster but also a teacher at Blackdom's "colored" school.

THE BLACK MENACE

The idea that there was a need to tame the "Black menace" led to the city of Roswell hiring Oscar Dowl, a well-known brute of a man, as a police officer. According to a January 4, 1918, article, "Pate Standifer, for several months' special city policeman, has been replaced by Oscar Dowl, who served the city during the Christmas rush. Dowl is well known here, having lived here for a number of years."[58] On January 5, the *Roswell Daily Record* reported that among the felony prosecutions taking place, Dowl faced charges of assault with a deadly weapon. According to Dowl, "a negro whom he arrested charged that Dowl beat him with a loaded stick."[59] After being relieved of duty in November 1918, "Dowl shot and killed Onie Reynolds," a White citizen of Roswell.[60] The city's escalation of propaganda against the "Black menace" progressively lessened over the course of 1918 after the Dowl case.

The "Black menace" was not completely excluded from Roswell's newspaper in the post–World War I era after 1918, but there was a significant retreat from the constant targeting of Black people with stories showing their inability to be productive in civil society. There were more stories of the "noble Black savage" that year. For example, the Jezebel caricature of Black women like Mittie Moore and Dixie Porter was offset with the caricature of Black women as "Mammy"—the ultimate of all the Black patriots—asexual and usually older women. In a front-page article, a *Roswell Daily Record* headline referred to the "Negro Woman Doing Her Share of War Work."[61]

According to the article, "No one has paid much attention to what the negro mammies and educated black women of America are doing to help win the war, but they're doing their share just the same. Paralleling the work and organizations of white women in the Southern branches of the Woman's Committee of the Council of National Defense, the colored women are keeping even, and in some instances a jump or two ahead of the procession. It is not that the Mammy caricature did not exist in 1917." The *Roswell Daily Record* reported on Mmes. S. M. Boyer, L. H. Henderson, E. K. Allen, and Harriet Smith, among others, who worked as a Red Cross unit of Blackdom "doing fine work" knitting scrubs for the war effort.[62] However, the stories were overshadowed by the crusade of Mayor Mullis to rid the Roswell streets of the "Black menace."

1919 BLACKDOM OIL COMPANY

Blackdom boasted having the first Black US Commissioner, Wesley T. Williams, in the area, as well attorney George Malone. The witnesses on Erastus Herron's final homestead proof attested to Herron's integrity underscored by the fact that he had two sons in the Army in France and took good care of the few children still at home. His wife testified that the family moved to the settlement in February 1915. In 1915, while in the midst of a Supreme Court case, Mittie began homestead No. 032454 in association with Blackdom. The Department of the Interior, US Land Office at Roswell, New Mexico, informed the public that Mittie was a legitimate landowner in Blackdom on August 29, 1919.[63] Twenty days earlier, a "New York company was blocking acreage at Blackdom and locating a site for the test well is expected to be in township."

On New Year's Eve 1919, the *Roswell Daily Record* published the headline "Will Pool Acreage," describing the actions of Blackdom residents. According to the article:

> The Blackdom people are making final arrangements to pool their land and it is all they expect to have in excess of 10,000 acres. This

land is to be put in a Roswell bank and kept there until some drilling company comes along with an acceptable proposition. The reports on the street that the National Exploration Co. had secured this land and were preparing to block it with their Orchard Park holding, are without foundation.[64]

CHAPTER 6

AFROTOPIA

BOOMTIMES

Blackdom Townsite was a real place and Blackdom Oil Company is a new Black history. My brother, Maison Nelson, and Dr. Kenneth Hamilton, my academic idol, both used the phrase "making things up" to describe the history I spent twenty years developing. Far from offended, I take seriously the idea that history can be manipulated and "made up." This chapter explores the public record of Blackdom Oil Company and the significant impact of the seminal finding. Intentionally, this chapter maintains minimal analysis to emphasize the mundanity of documents to produce a thorough accounting. Blackdom's renaissance as a township movement morphed into a place of oil exploration and produced royalties for Blackdomites.

BLACKDOM AND BLACKDOM OIL COMPANY (1919–1930)

Oil exploration during the 1910s in Southeastern New Mexico earned the regional space the nickname "Little Texas." Commercialization of oil exploration allowed Blackdom to fully engage the regional economy during the Roaring Twenties and the Harlem Renaissance. Blackdom's early years were plagued with drought and lack of full participation. By 1918, those who proved up land were on the verge of economic sovereignty. Prospects for an oil boom in the region increased the urgency of Black folks seeking to homestead. Women of Blackdom were a vital component in the new era of Blackdom signified in the increase of their land holdings, led by Ella Boyer who completed her 160-acre patent on land adjacent to Blackdom's forty-acre town square (land patented by her husband, Frank). Blackdom was New Mexico's only all-Black town and its inhabitants entered into contracts with oil exploration companies that leased their homestead land. Oil was first discovered in New Mexico in 1907 and commercial wells began in 1922.

In 1919, Blackdomites benefited from the speculation bubble in the region when the homestead class incorporated the Blackdom Oil Company. Leaders in the collective were led by ministers, military personnel, Freemasons, and engineers from Blackdomite families (Boyer, Ragsdale, Eubank, Gates, and Collins, to name a few) who agreed to deposit their land with the Roswell Picacho Investment Co.—a bank twenty miles north of the town square. The new economic orientation led to the rise of the infamous Mittie Moore in Blackdom. Mittie homesteaded a whole square mile of land three miles south of Blackdom's town square. She struggled to meet proving-up requirements until she received help from a few influential people of the town in the fall of 1919. Mittie was the social antithesis of the original identity of Blackdom and her inclusion in the community was a point of transition.

In January 1920, Blackdomites announced in the *Roswell Daily Record*, "Will Drill at Blackdom," inviting wildcatters and other oil speculators to participate in the boom that promised riches for Blackdomites who had lands made available for oil drilling. The fury of advertisements for Blackdom Oil peaked by Juneteenth of 1920. By year's end, Blackdomites entered contracts with oil exploration companies from New York to California. On September 1, 1920, the *Roswell Daily Record* reported that an unidentified California syndicate had

"Made Location at Blackdom." Currently lost to history was how many wells and barrels Blackdomite lands produced.

Lasting prosperity materialized in Blackdom's outposts that were sustained by inter-commerce among families within a vast regional network of farmers, migrants, Masonic lodges, and churches, among other Black intersections. Eustace and Francis Jr., of the Boyer family, were a part of a WWI cohort of military men who proved up homesteads during the postwar period and grew their families. Committed to an Afrotopia underwritten by oil royalties, Frank Boyer left Chaves County and resettled in Vado, Doña Ana County, New Mexico, after completing the townsite's official plat in May 1920.

By 1930 and the start of the Great Depression, Blackdom succumbed to the winds of the Dust Bowl. Blackdom Oil, however, continued to produce royalties for the homestead class. Local newspapers reported that the Blackdom Oil Company continued business dealings. Kathryn Henry, a reporter for the *Clovis News-Journal*, reported the last known public interview with Frank Boyer in 1947 two years prior to his passing. Boyer was justice of the peace then and has been a justice for many years since. He and some of his associates organized what he believed was the only Negro oil company ever formed, the Lincoln Oil Co. The former residents of Blackdom are now scattered from Dallas to the Pacific Coast, but some of the stockholders of the original Lincoln Oil Company still own 100,000 acres of land which now is under lease to the Gulf Oil Co.[1]

Although reported as Lincoln Oil, the documented incorporation of the original name points to the Blackdom Oil Company. The name change came after increased racial tension, and "Blackdom" did little to shield the Afro-Frontierists behind the corporate veil. Nevertheless, Frank Boyer affirmed the new narrative that Blackdomites engaged in the regional bonanza during the Harlem Renaissance and the Roaring Twenties. Moreover, after the Great Depression, Black folks continued to earn royalties that flowed well into the post–World War II era. Afro-Frontierism, a keen sense of opportunity, and timing led Black folks from a dry utopia in 1903 through a period of boom times by 1923. By then, new Blackdomites fully shifted to a mostly extractive notion of their existence in Afrotopia. Blackdomites produced Black sovereignty and generational wealth that persisted even when the "township" died.

THE NEWS

Popular media included different publications, theater, and most important were daily newspapers. In 1919, Blackdomite families were fully thriving as a townsite with exponential growth in land mass during the early 1920s. Townsite residents were pleased to announce the new developments. On August 8, 1919, the *Roswell Daily Record* reported, "Activity In Drilling Now Near Artesia," "New York company was blocking acreage at Blackdom and locating a site for the test well is expected to be in the township thirteen-twenty-four."[2] The newspaper further reported, "It is announced that Lincoln has sold a 49 per cent interest in the Lincoln Oil company holdings including Lincoln well No. 1 for $300,000, said purchase being made by six California investors, who took $50,000 each."[3] Blackdom became a part of the extremely competitive bonanza in this borderland region.

To fully grasp the dynamism of Blackdomites, one must recognize that they occupied two spaces at the same time. The exact population at any point in Blackdom's history was elusive because Blackdomites were transient. According to the 1920 census, Chaves County had 12,075 residents, of which 191 were Black, 6 men and 4 women were illiterate. Half of the Black population was female.[4] There were 102 "Negro" families, 78 of which had no children in Chaves County. Although the census calculates a small population; also, the census takers and administration are known to have manipulated data and undercounted to appease a racialization narrative in the newly created state. During the 1920s, the county had a mostly adult, literate, mobile, cash infused Black population who consumed, articulated and produced new knowledge in contributions to an intersectional Black consciousness.

On December 31, 1919, the *Roswell Daily Record* reported, "the Blackdom people are making final arrangements to pool their land," was the start of a new phase in Blackdom's history.[5] Alchemically, Blackdomites had created Afrotopia. Landowners in the Afro-Frontier town had public financial success, and redemption.[6] Black people created Black power in a New Mexican County founded by ex-confederates. Owning the assets of the Blackdom Oil Company made money in two main ways—by the selling of stock in the company and leasing the land.[7] The bank (Roswell Picacho Investment Company) made money certifying, commoditizing, and capitalizing on Blackdom's land and brokering deals. The drilling company paid an agreed upon amount to the Blackdom Oil Company, which was then dispersed among the partners. Oil resulting from the exploration was an asset of the oil drilling company wherein the drilling company paid royalties to Blackdomites.[8]

Separate-and-equal, Blackdom in boom times was a dual reality for all who engaged in Afrotopia for a few reasons. Most notably, eventually, Black people would be faced with the condition of Blackness in public. With no known documents of private conversations, I rely on the wisdom of my grandfather, Daddy Glen, to contextualize the Blackdomite dilemma: "White folks don't like to see Black folks doing better than them." In other words, Black folks' success often bred envy in neighboring communities. New Mexican statehood had many effects, some more advantageous than others. Specifically, power over the legal apparatus of the "state" guaranteed a decade of increased challenges inside the corporate veil of a Black municipality. Chaves County began as a Confederate stronghold and became an outpost of White supremacy. Blackdomite success proved difficult to reconcile with the cultural hegemonic notion of Whiteness in Roswell. Blackdom's power produced a "Whitelash" that helped to bury the existence of the Blackdom Oil Company.

A month before the Blackdom Oil Company announcement, the "Roswell Oil Development Company sold 500,000 Acres To Big Concern."[9] The "Concern" was that the sale of that much land would kill the smaller market oil companies in the area. According to the report:

> The biggest oil deal ever made in New Mexico was closed last night when H. A. Houser, of Los Angeles, on behalf of the National Exploration Company of New York City, purchased more than 500,000 acres of leases from the Roswell Oil Development Company. It is believed that this transaction means the beginning of real development for oil in eastern New Mexico.[10]

Land owning Blackdomites empowered themselves to compete. Oil and speculation "moneys" were finite resources and a point of competition. "The purchase price was not definitely announced, but it was admitted being more than $350,000."[11] According to the report, "when it is all in they [Blackdom Oil Company] expect to have in excess of 10,000 acres. This land is to be put in a Roswell bank and kept there until some drilling company comes along with an acceptable proposition. The reports on the street that the National Exploration Co. had secured this land and were preparing to block it with their Orchard Park holdings are without foundation."[12]

Guided by biblical principles, the early investors in the township of Blackdom did so based on the notions of a regenerative society and a sense of finality after the Day of Jubilee. The next generation of Blackdomites were a cohort of travelers, many of whom understood "Blackdom" through the lens of utility, extraction, and colonization. Blackdom's boom times brought about a rift in Blackdom's Afrotopia as sovereignty produced the effect of divided leadership, loyalties, and expectations. Blackdomites all maintained a second existence away from the Blackdom town square. As the newer homestead class began to outnumber the older, Blackdomite culture shifted into the city of Roswell and dispersed across the world as Blackdomite children continued to seek sovereignty through migration and colonization.

There were a few families who continued to engage "Blackdom" as an agricultural utopia: specifically, Crutcher Eubank of the Eubank family. Nevertheless, January 1, 1920, marked Blackdom as a real place in boom times. Arguably, few knew global markets were headed towards a Great Depression. For Blackdomites, the Roaring Twenties was a test of differing sovereign paths. Blown away in the Dust Bowl, the Afrotopic Blackdom vaporized; existing only in the form of currency/royalty for Blackdom's homestead class into the WWII period and possibly beyond.

BLACKDOM OIL NEWS

In March 1920, Blackdom Oil Company entered a land leasing contract with the National Exploration Company for 4,200 acres of land. The members of the Blackdom Oil Company received a "bonus of $1.25 an acre." To drill in Blackdom, oilmen bought contracts and, once the money was deposited in the bank, had a ninety-day window to begin operations. The Blackdom Oil Company offered land for $15 ($200 today) an acre. Who the leaders were, and how the money was distributed, has yet to be discovered. Provided that money was distributed according to the number of acres one homesteaded, the system appeared formulaic. Most individuals owned one hundred sixty acres or less and no one was legally allowed to own more than six hundred forty acres.[13]

In March 1920, Blackdom was "To Sink a Deep Roswell Well." According to an *El Paso Times* article, "A Buffalo group of oil men have signed a contract with the Blackdom Oil company for the drilling of a deep test on 4200 acres 12 miles south of this city." The Blackdom Oil Company was begun: "Under the terms of the contract, drilling is to commence within 90 days." Also included in the contract, "The hole must be started with a 20-inch casing and put down to a depth of 3500\feet, unless oil or gas is found a paying quantities at a lesser depth. Martin Yates, Jr., of Artesia, has lately signed a contract with a California drilling company for a deep test north of Lake Arthur." Blackdom Oil was the second contract made in Chaves County within the past thirty days. "The Cumberland Park Oil company hopes to sign a contract for a deep test just south of Orchard Park within the next few days." Lastly, "Two drills of the National Exploration company are now pounding into the ground and another is ready to start within the next twenty-five days. Oil enthusiasm here continues to grow." Blackdom was booming and Chaves County was the area of choice for oil exploration in the region.

In April 1920, Blackdom was under contract for another deep well test.[14] The residents of the town won a contract with the National Exploration Company—one of the larger mid-continent drilling companies. According to the agreement, drilling had to begin no later than June 6, 1920. Black people in Blackdom had watched as the town declined economically during the second decade, and in the third decade the same worthless land provided compensation from multinational corporations, which brought them bonuses of $1,000 ($13,400 today) and a bond of $5,000 ($200,000 today) deposited by the drilling company "to show good faith."

In 1920, Blackdom's economic outlook was healthy. The economic vision for the Afro-Frontier town of Blackdom crystalized on September 1, 1920, "Blackdom Location Made." According to the *Roswell Daily Record*:

> The location for the deep test well at Blackdom south of this city has just been made. This well will be drilled a quarter of a mile west of Blackdom and the derrick is now under construction. The well will be put down by a California syndicate, represented here by Verne Lincoln. A rotary rig will be used to go the first 1,000 feet and excellent progress is expected.[15]

The existence of the Blackdom Oil Company upset the racial order by allowing for the social mobility of Black people, which vaulted them ahead of many Roswell elites. In November, the Blackdom Oil Company announced that there was interest in another Blackdom well.[16]

BLACKDOM AND THE HARLEM RENAISSANCE

In November 1920, Blackdomites were in full Afrotopia, and started to read about themselves in *The Crisis* magazine. From Artesia, New Mexico, Ruth Loomis Skeen's letter to W.E.B. Du Bois prompted the magazine to publish an article about Blackdom:

> Near here [Artesia, New Mexico] is a settlement of Negroes—a little town called "Blackdom", consisting of farmers who have wrenched every bit of good out of our bitter soil. They are quiet, good citizens and molest nobody. They have had little chance for the cultural things of life and I believe they welcome an opportunity to take your papers and magazines. Of course, they may already know about them. They have a little school and a church.
>
> Once in Omaha, I had an argument with a man who insisted that any woman's life was in danger who went alone on the streets of the city after night. I maintained that the danger would be from thugs or mashers. I have been accosted by white mashers on the city streets, but I have never been noticed by Negroes. In order to prove my point, I offered to walk the length of Cumings Street alone after nine o'clock. It is a street upon which a large number of colored people live, presumably of the worst class. For three nights I walked home the length of this street before boarding the street car for Pinkney, and met man after man of colored race without the slightest effort on his part to even turn and look after me.[17]

Curiously, Ruth Loomis Skeen did not mention the Blackdom Oil Company.

With Blackdom as a source of income—that is, royalties—Frank and Ella Boyer, Daniel Keys, and other townspeople were no longer obligated to remain on the land on which they toiled and began a new Afrotopia in Vado, New Mexico. The unincorporated community became a new space from which to read about "Blackdom." Frank frequently traveled back to Blackdom and Roswell to visit family, attend Masonic meetings, and to pick up his royalty checks. Blackdom's church was built during the height of Blackdom's revival in 1915. In the summer of 1922, Blackdomites sold the church house to First United Methodist Church of Cottonwood, 15 miles south of Blackdom. By then, Blackdomites had established a "Negro" church in Roswell. As a town, Blackdom slowly declined in population as Blackdomite families leased their land to oil exploration companies. The business of Blackdom moved to Roswell, and Blackdom's town square became a ceremonial place to celebrate major events like Juneteenth.

BLACKDOM OIL COMPANY | *ROSWELL DAILY RECORD* DECEMBER 31, 1919: "WILL DRILL AT BLACKDOM," *ROSWELL DAILY RECORD*, FRIDAY, APRIL 16, 1920

Blackdom was a town that enforced temperance and shortly after the announcement of Blackdom Oil Company, Blackdom faithful began a new exodus outward as new leadership of the town focused their efforts on extraction instead of regenerative agricultural practices. Blackdom's Boom Time began and ended in the Roaring Twenties when the town's economy shifted from agriculture to oil exploration. Unfettered boldness and progress led Blackdomites to secured futures backed by oil royalties. The new Blackdom moved town business to Roswell where Blackdomite children grew up knowing the hostility of White folks. Although affluent, Black people in Chaves County were increasingly threatened.

In December 1919, the *Roswell Daily Record* reported the incorporation of the Blackdom Oil Company with land holdings of 10,000 acres. The new age in Blackdom ushered in a host of new leaders including Blackdomite men who returned from WWI and an infamous bootlegging madam named Mittie Moore (Wilson). As the 1920s approached, Mittie had become public enemy no. 1 in Chaves County as she significantly financially benefited from Roswell and

Blackdom. As oil speculation increased, so too increased the perceived success of Black people and a hypervisibility and Mittie's inclusion in the Blackdom community was a signal of leadership and priority for the Afro-Frontier town.

Unlike any other Notice for Publication, the *Roswell Daily Record* printed Mittie's notice every day for the month of September and part of October in 1919. Mittie's life and her public persona as an "unscrupulous" figure was officially linked to the Blackdom community and Blackdom Oil Company.

In order to complete the patent process, one needed four witnesses to testify that one "proved up" the land. Moreso, the witnesses testified to the "good" character of the homesteader. Joe Blue of Blackdom, Clinton Ragsdale of Blackdom, Henry Smith of Blackdom, and Erasmus Herron of Blackdom were signatories for Mittie's final homestead proving-up documents. Moore's witnesses signified the new leadership at Blackdom Townsite.

The notice was the first documented proof that Mittie was a part of Blackdom's "community." Adding Mittie's land to the total land mass of Blackdom increased the ability to secure drilling contracts. One cannot overstate the inherent tension that comes as a result of the interaction between the first cohort of deeply religious Blackdomites and the incoming wave of more extractive oriented Blackdomites. The first Blackdomites understood Blackdom through the lens of Afrotopia. Ella and Frank's relocation near the Rio Grande River in Vado was to continue their understanding of township and sovereignty. Nevertheless, they all intersected at the profit motive.

By 1920, there was a coordinated effort by Blackdom residents to make money from the oil boom, and an increased effort, on the part of people in the city of Roswell, to dehumanize Blackdom residents and Black people. The *Roswell Daily Record* began a new era of hostility towards Mittie after the printing of her homestead patent notice. Oil companies were notoriously corrupt and Blackdom's direct connection with Mittie and her bawdy reputation had the possibility to sabotage investment opportunities. Oil speculation was a well-known risky venture, and many people were scammed.

1919 THE NETWORK

Moore's witnesses were leaders and residents of the Blackdom Townsite. Nick Gates was a witness on Herron's final proof and was questioned in the investigation on February 8, 1919. Special agent Mason Leming interviewed Gates on his homestead less than a mile away from Herron. Gates stood by his argument that he witnessed Herron cultivate twelve acres. When the questioning intensified, Herron made the statement that the judge got "tangled up," or did not quite understand. Gates did attest to the fact that he saw the Herron homestead at least once a week for years. George Malone was postmaster as well as teacher at Blackdom's "colored" school. Malone was interviewed in the Erastus Herron's homestead case. The interview took place at the post office of Blackdom Townsite. Malone stated that Herron lived on his homestead for at least nine years. Malone with his family settled in Blackdom September of 1915 and was a boarder hosted by the Herron family. From 1915 to the time of the investigation, Malone stated that all he witnessed was continuous residence on the part of the Herron family.

After 1919, there was an increased effort to finish homestead patents, but also start new ones as Erastus completed his second homestead in 1924. The détente in the assaults on the Black image in Roswell was short lived when Blackdom became the center for oil speculation. Shortly after Roswell's economic and population boom during World War I, Black people became hyper-visible.

The incorporation of the Blackdom Oil Company made possible Black folks' engagement. By 1922, oil speculation was at a fever pitch with additional discoveries in Artesia and San Juan Counties. Possibly Blackdomites understood the rise of oil exploration. As early as 1915, while in the midst of a Supreme Court case, Mittie began homestead No. 032454 in association with Blackdom. The Department of the Interior, US Land Office at Roswell, New Mexico, informed the public that Mittie was a legitimate landowner in Blackdom on August 29, 1919. Twenty days earlier, a "New York company was blocking acreage at Blackdom and locating a site for the test well is expected to be in township." Blackdomites, including Mittie, intensified their efforts to complete the homestead prior to the official announcement in December of 1919 and accelerated after January of 1920.

The old Blackdom narrative articulates the demise when, "The Boyers left the Pecos Valley around 1920." For many scholars, Frank's departure signaled failure, however, the Blackdom Thesis identifies his move as a transition point. Instead, Blackdom's success and new money allowed Blackdomites to venture beyond the borders of the township and further extend their network. Frank's oil royalties allowed him to operate hundreds of miles away from Blackdom on fertile, easy-to-irrigate land in Doña Ana County. At the same time, Frank maintained investments in Blackdom directly, familial businesses, and fraternal ties to Chaves County. The Afro-Frontier network in the Borderlands continued to broaden amongst ministers, military personnel, and Freemasons. The Great Depression destabilized the physical Blackdom, but the teachings in churches and exchange of ideas in lodges carried on the dynamism with Blackdomites in diaspora.

Prior to the Blackdom Oil Company, Black people operated in Chaves County without serious threats from institutionalized racial violence. After the announcement of the Blackdom Oil Company, White rage slowly grew in their tabernacles and social clubs. The people of Roswell hosted a Ku Klux Klan (KKK) movement that manifested into the establishment of a chapter in Roswell. The importance of a network of Black folk went beyond cautionary and became insurance against the eccentricities of White supremacists' notions.

A NARRATIVE RECONCILIATION

Frank Boyer's move out of Chaves County around 1920 coincided with the US nationwide campaign of White violence directed towards Black people, specifically financially successful Black communities. Blackdom had become a financial success; Frank, and others, understood the racial climate in the country, and the county. By moving, Frank provided a safe space in case one needed to start over. Frank's migration magnified an Afro-Frontier network that had already existed from Columbus, New Mexico to El Paso, Texas through various military posts, Black churches, and Masonic lodges along the US–Mexico border.

Frank and Ella's time in Chaves County shows they endured a tremendous amount of transition as their investments matured and sometimes failed. Simultaneously, their consistent migration exposed them to different conversations about the land they inhabited and its potential. While Frank and Ella were living in Lake Arthur, about fifteen miles south of the Blackdom townsite, oil exploration entered popular conversation.

There was significant investment in homesteads associated with Blackdom before 1919, particularly after the second generation of Blackdom residents matured. Blackdom was in transition in 1920 rather than popular notions of decline. Frank Boyer left Chaves County after finalizing Blackdom's existence, as his sons and other family as well as community members assumed the position of furthering the growth of the town's business. Blackdom remained.

In April 1920, Boyer was a Final Homestead Proof Witness for Loney Wagoner along with Clinton Ragsdale, John Woodard, and Jack Wagoner. There was still coordination among Blackdom residents, especially prominent members of the community. Loney Wagoner was one of the newer residents, who began his homestead in July of 1915. While homesteading, he needed to build some capital, and he left his homestead in January and did not return to work as a farm hand for A.D. Hill in Lake Arthur. He often left for months working for different farmers in the county as well as neighboring counties. On April 15, 1920, Loney Wagoner of Blackdom received his Notice of Publication from the Department of the Interior approved by the US Land Office at Roswell for his homestead. Loney was one of a growing cohort of new Blackdomites. In 1919, the advent of the Blackdom Oil

Company represented a new era and a third decade emerged in a new Blackdom history.

THE NEWS

The intensity of the moment included the potential of oil revenues. The *Roswell Daily Record*, on August 8, 1919, under the heading, "Activity in Drilling Now Near Artesia," reported that a "New York company was blocking acreage at Blackdom and locating a site for the test well is expected to be in the township thirteen-twenty-four."[18] The newspaper further reported, "It is announced that Lincoln has sold a 49 per cent interest in the Lincoln Oil company holdings including Lincoln well No. 1 for $300,000, said purchase being made by six California investors, who took $50,000 each." Blackdom was competitive in a regional bonanza.

In January 1919, the *Roswell Daily Record* announced, "Much Local Interest Being Shown In the Great Ranger, Texas Oil Field."[19] According to the article, Oil is again one of the chief topics of conversation on the streets of this city. Not even in the days when the Toltec company was drilling north of Roswell, have people generally become so excited over oil and oil news. A number of Roswell men have had the good fortune to own or later to become interested in the oil field at Ranger, Eastland Co., Texas This field already promises to be one of the largest in the country and has made dollars for a number of Roswell men.

The announcement that "the Blackdom people are making final arrangements to pool their land coincided with a wave of positive oil news.[20] Exciting people in Roswell, "This morning for the fourth time in the past thirty days a number of Roswell people received dividend checks for royalty interests in the Ranger Oil Field." Moreover, these royalties amounted to "forty percent of the original investment." In January 1919, Big Ten Oil Company sought to expand in Chaves County, starting in March and announced that if one was "Out of Oil Investments in Wichita County Texas GET YOUR PART OF IT," with the new drilling for $10 a share. The advertisement was half a page. To help build credibility, the company emphasized that the trustee John Peck, who first had to be "at the bedside of his mother who has been very sick but who is now much improved. After a few days here Mr. Peck will leave for Wichita Falls, Texas where he will personally oversee the drilling on the Big Ten Oil Co. holdings."[21]

In direct competition with the Big Ten Oil Company, the Roswell Oil Development Company offered itself as the more solid investment. In a March 1919 article, company directors urged the public to first consider the Roswell Oil Development Company, which has "approximately 200,000 acres of leases for oil development."[22] According to the article, "It should have the support, of entry land owner, and there is no better opportunity today to get quick development in which land owners and the public generally will share than this. Land owners are therefore urged to see this company before signing leases."

On August 8, 1919, the *Roswell Daily Record* reported that near Artesia there was "the big drilling outfit shipped from El Dorado, Kans., by the Kansas–New Mexico Oil company, arrived at Lakewood Saturday and has been erected about 20 miles southeast, and active drilling work will commence as soon as the derrick is up and the machinery is installed."[23] Also, "Another drilling outfit from El Dorado, to be shipped by the Eddy county Oil and Gas company is expected to follow soon.

1920 LOCATION MADE AT BLACKDOM

The city of Roswell increased policing parallel with the formation of the Blackdom Oil Company. The story of Blackdom Oil Company indicates a more significant Blackdom history at a time when Frank Boyer was no longer a major fixture in the town. The new era of hypervisibility factored into how Black people in Chaves County engaged outside of the corporate veil.

There were many other oil companies mentioned in Roswell throughout 1919—Toltec, Roebuck, Felix River, Lincoln, Kribs, Elver,

Carter, and Black-Burnett, to mention a few in the first three months of the year. At the same time, most of the reports ended with reports like, "Roebuck a Dry Hole." In the first half of 1919, daily newspapers in Roswell fed the fervor. By May, exhaustion with the oil speculation bubble led to stories focused on rebuilding confidence in the city's oil boom. The *Roswell Daily Record* encouraged the city with articles such as, "Things Moving in the Roswell Big Oil Field." According to the article:

> There are more oil men coming to Roswell today than ever before, according to those in touch with the situation. And that despite the fact that most people feel that the "oil excitement" has waned. The excitement has cooled, because what was unusual two months ago is now commonplace. A geologist caused a furor a few months ago—they live here now. The interest in the Roswell field is increasing all over the country. Inquiries are coming from practically every state.[24]

In the first half of 1919, there was a significant number of ads for a plethora of oil companies to invest in—Felix River Oil Company (Eddy County), Lincoln Oil Company (Lincoln County), and Roswell Oil Development Company (Chaves County) to mention a few.[25] The daily newspaper in Roswell promoted prospecting, "Even though we know tis a gamble don't you think it worth trying for?"[26] In March, the *Roswell Daily Record* explicitly stated, "The object of this article is simply to pass on the government warning."[27]

Most people who invested in oil lost money, so much so that by August 1919 the US Congress drafted legislation to limit speculation in unproven oil fields. Accordingly, this tendency was noted: on "[o]il Drilling in Pecos Valley, there is a matter up before Congress now which is of vital interest to the people of Eddy County says the *Carlsbad Current* in a recent issue. It is the bill relating to the disposal of the oilbearing lands belonging in the public domain." It went on to state that "[t]he biggest concern was that there is hardly anyone in Carlsbad who has not at one time or another had his or her name on one of these placer claims, and who did not hope to get rich thereby. So far no one has yet made any mint of gold from them, but they have been the only means of taking possession of mineral-bearing lands in the public domain. A leasing law is now before Congress, which will limit the amount of mineral land one man may own to twenty-five hundred and sixty acres in an unproven field, or to six hundred and forty in a proven field."[28]

Meanwhile, Blackdomite families including the Boyer, Collins, Herron, Proffit, and Ragsdale, among others, continued to build Blackdom while firmly establishing themselves outside the boundaries of Blackdom. Ester and Ura Herron completed their homestead patents prior to 1919. Ulysses and Wedie Herron followed them and completed their homestead patent processes in 1920. The Volstead Act made it illegal to produce, transport, or sell alcohol; the act passed in January of 1919 and became effective in January 1920. Mittie was a chronic offender. On August 30, 1929, the *Roswell Daily Record* reported that "Mittie Moore Wilson, local negress," was being "Held On Liquor Charge."[29]

In 1920, after a year of relative calm, the *Roswell Daily Record* once again published stories such as "Police Capture 11 in Big Raid."[30] This was an article about the "Black menace" in Roswell. According to the article:

> Chief-of-Police R. W. Corman, assisted by B. F. Leonard, raided the negro pool hall on South Main street Saturday night and when the final vote was taken it was found that eleven victims had found their way into the police net. This hall has been under superbision [*sic*] of the police for some time, but it was only on Saturday night when the signs were right and the raid was made.[31]

Lynching as well as Black social deviance was back on the front page of the local daily newspaper. In a more localized display of racialization and pathologizing Black bodies, there was an increased police presence in the form of vagrancy citations. Four of the eleven men at the pool hall were charged with vagrancy. These four were each given a fine of $10 and "the fine was suspended on payment of the costs."[32] The others were charged with gambling and fined $50. Before 1917, there were very few if any vagrancy charges filed against Black people. After 1919, there was a significant increase.

Over the course of 1920, the *Roswell Daily Record* continued to inundate the public with stories about Blackdom as animosity built up in Roswell towards Black people. Drilling for oil in Blackdom soon became a national story. On April 11, the *Fort Worth Star-Telegram* published a piece called "New Mexico Going Hard After Oil; New Test Daily." According to the article,

> With three new locations for deep tests made in Eastern New Mexico during the past week, the interest in oil development keeps up its pace. The wells already started are all making excellent progress with every indication that the existence of oil in this section of the Sunshine State will be proved or disproved by the middle of the Summer. A contract has just been signed here between the Blackdom Oil Company and the Mescalero Oil Company for a deep test eleven miles south of this city on what is known as Blackdom Dome. The contract calls for this well to start by July 1. Machinery and equipment are already in transit. The National Exploration Company has made its fourth location six miles southwest of this city on what is known as "Six Mile" hill and the derrick is now erected. This well is to start not later than June 1. All the machinery is now on the drilling site.[33]

Roswell was saturated with advertisements from the Roswell Picacho Investment Co., offering commercial leases of land in Blackdom at $15 per acre, which for Mittie meant about $10,000 if she leased all 640 acres of her land.

1921 THE NEXT GENERATION OF THE BOYER FAMILY HOMESTEAD

Velma, Erastus, and Durand Herron completed their homesteads in 1921. Erastus and Durand applied for more homestead land and completed the process in 1924. As a family, they owned close to twenty-two hundred acres of land. Meanwhile, Frank and Ella Boyer, Daniel Keys and other townspeople began a new Afrotopia two hundred miles away from Blackdom. As noted, Frank frequently traveled to Blackdom and Roswell to visit family, attend Masonic meetings and to pick up his royalty checks. Many of the first wave of religious Blackdomites who stayed in Chaves County moved to Roswell. Blackdom's church was built during the height of Blackdom's revival in 1915. During Blackdom's Boom Time, on February 25, 1922, Mittie completed a second homestead proving documents for a whole square mile on the south side of Blackdom commons.

Shortly after, in the summer of 1922, Blackdomites sold the church house to First United Methodist Church of Cottonwood fifteen miles south of Blackdom. By then, Blackdomites had established a negro church in Roswell. Thomas Collins senior applied for a second patent and received his land rights in 1919 followed by William in 1922. Oil speculation fueled the land grab and the rise in White supremacy as competition for drilling contracts reached larger regional audiences with additional discoveries in Artesia and San Juan Counties.[34] In 1915, while in the midst of a Supreme Court case, Mittie began homestead No. 032454 in association with Blackdom. The Department of the Interior, US Land Office at Roswell, New Mexico, informed the public that Mittie was a legitimate landowner in Blackdom on August 29, 1919.[35] Twenty days earlier, a "New York company was blocking acreage at Blackdom and locating a site for the test well is expected to be in township."[36] Blackdom was far from abandoned when Frank Boyer left Chaves County.

Mistakenly, in June 1922, the *Artesia Advocate* reported, "An experiment in the colonization of the Negro, which was attempted several years ago at the little village of Blackdom, has proven to be a failure." Failure had not occurred in 1922: Blackdom was in transition due in part to the new economic position and hypervisibility. Blackdom served its original purpose, and the new purpose required a lower profile. Part of Blackdom's transition was selling the Blackdom Baptist Church to residents in Cottonwood (near Lake Arthur) ten miles north of Artesia.

In Roswell, there was a "Colored Methodist Episcopal Church" as well as a "Colored Baptist Church." "Blackdom" migrated with the people and was most vivid in Blackdom's town square. The Blackdom Oil Company pushed Blackdomites out of Afrotopia and into Roswell where Black people were increasingly vulnerable. The dual existence of Blackdom residents and Roswell's invisible workforce yielded little attention for the Black population as a whole. The Blackdomite families (Boyers, Herrons, Collins, Proffits, and Ragsdales) continued to build "Blackdom" as Black folks did before them, in churches, military ranks, and Masonic lodges.

In Dexter, the Boyers hosted the Collins family for their first six months. In 1907, Blackdom inspired Monroe and Mary Collins who migrated from Mississippi to be Blackdomites. Blackdom was a new beginning with freedoms and no Jim Crow laws in the territory. Peter Collins was the first to earn a homestead patent as early as 1909. The Collins family endured the last of Lost Year's and grew their land holding during Blackdom Revival. In 1914, Monroe and Thomas Collins completed their homestead patent process, followed by Peter's second homestead in 1915. Frederick Collins in 1916, and Thomas E. (son of Thomas) completed his patent in 1917. Thomas senior applied for a second patent and received his land rights in 1919 followed by William in 1922. The Blackdom vision continued into the 1920s with families seeking to own miles of land in Chaves County.

During the Roaring Twenties in Chaves County, New Mexico, Black people were in a renaissance with tangible means of expression. In

"Imperial Outpost on the Border: El Paso's Frontier and Klan," Shawn Lay described the development of the Ku Klux Klan (KKK). According to Lay, Texas was fruitful ground for recruitment and "When the KKK arrived in 1921, with its solemn vow to 'strive for the eternal maintenance of white supremacy,' the secret order found a ready audience." Very little has been written about the KKK in New Mexico; however, it was during the time when Blackdom became the center of Roswell's economic boom that the KKK appeared in Roswell.

In 1921, the *Roswell Daily Record* continued an ongoing narrative about resurgence of the KKK across the United States, but specifically focused attention on neighboring Texas. The KKK and the old Confederate states were a part of daily discussions mostly due to an increase in stories. The *Roswell Daily Record* reported, "Confederate Veteran Dead." According to the article, "a resident of Texas seventy-six years and leader of the Ku Klux Klan in Limestone County during the post-war and reconstruction days, and a confederate Veteran, died in a sanitarium at Marin." The Ku Klux Klan was never a major force in New Mexico, but they quickly grew as a force in Roswell after 1920. The announcement that "the Blackdom people are making final arrangements to pool their land" was the start of a new phase of White supremacy efforts.

1922 BLACKDOMITE EXODUS

By 1922, the oil speculation was at a fever pitch with additional discoveries in Artesia and San Juan Counties.[37] Thomas senior applied for a second patent and received his land rights in 1919 followed by William in 1922. Essentially, Blackdom served its purpose, not as a refuge, but an investment vehicle from which the residents/investors withdrew their profits after a maturation period of almost twenty years for some of them.

As mentioned, in June of 1922 the *Artesia Advocate* mistakenly reported, "An experiment in the colonization of the Negro, which was attempted several years ago at the little village of Blackdom, has proven to be a failure." In reality, failure had not occurred by 1922, but Blackdom was in transition because of economic stability. Nineteen horses hauled away the church and the singular most significant artifact of the original Blackdom. In doing so, there was little ability to target Blackdomites with mass racial violence. Longevity required strategy, and most Blackdomites were keenly aware of the violent South they migrated from. With Frank, Ella and a host of other Blackdomites, an exodus allowed Blackdom Oil Company to grow while going somewhat unnoticed by most outside observers.

The Boyer, Herron, Collins, Proffit, and Ragsdale families continued to build "Blackdom" though most of their time was spent in Roswell. Ester and Ura Herron completed their homestead patents prior to 1919. Ulysses and Wedie Herron followed and completed their homestead patent processes in 1920. Velma, Erastus, and Durand Herron completed their homesteads in 1921. Erastus and Durand applied for more homestead land and completed the process in 1924. As a family, the Herrons owned close to twenty-two hundred acres of land.

1923 WHITELASH

On September 13, 1923, the *Roswell Daily Record* reported that "Albuquerque Klan Meets." The article offers confirmation of the existence of the KKK in New Mexico, specifically Roswell. Moreover, the Roswell chapter that developed in 1924 "had been perfected in the city of Albuquerque."[38] The *Farmington Times Hustler* reported on September 7, 1923, "Las Vegas [New Mexico] Hit By Flood Of Ku Klux Klan Circulars."[39] The vast majority of the infinitesimal Black population was concentrated in these three cities as well as in Deming and Las Cruces, in part, because of the significant amount of Black soldiers stationed in those areas. All of these cites faced the threat of the KKK, even though they maintained an enemies list that went beyond the Black population, particularly Catholics.

"Americanism" became the core of marketing the KKK. On December 12, 1924, the District Attorney of Gainesville, Texas, Fred E.

Wankan, and a KKK representative gave a lecture on "Americanism."[40] Wankan was introduced by Frank Talmage. "Dr. E. T. Wilson, of the Seventh Day Adventists, first announced that the Adventists had given the use of the tabernacle to the Klan when asked for it, because they believed a lecture on 'Americanism' could not be bad. He disclaimed any affiliation with the Klan on the part of his membership." Wanken was grateful because the authorities of the Amory rejected him. The crowd packed the building "judging from the applause which was given the speaker, generally approved of his declaration."[41] Frederick Sager, pastor of the First Methodist Episcopal Church opened the meeting with a prayer.

In November 1923, it was reported that Mittie was "In District Court . . . charged with possession of intoxicating liquor, is on trial today before Judge Charles R. Brice in district court. This case is an appeal from the justice court." Elvis Fleming (Archivist in Roswell) noted that no records indicate exactly when the Roswell Klan came together, but believed it was around 1923.

On September 13, 1923, the *Roswell Daily Record* reported that "Albuquerque Klan Meets." The article offers confirmation of the existence of the KKK in New Mexico, specifically Roswell. Moreover, the Roswell chapter that developed in 1924 "had been perfected in the city of Albuquerque." The Farmington Times Hustler reported on September 7, 1923, "Las Vegas [New Mexico] Hit By Flood Of Ku Klux Klan Circulars." KKK charted at New Mexico's legal institutions, schools and colleges, and all "civil society" through marketing, recruitment and strategic placement of those loyal to the Klan.

1924 PIONEER KLAN NO. 15

Southeastern New Mexico began as a Southern-styled Confederate society and some Roswellians embraced "Christian" lectures that promoted the Ku Klux Klan. In 1924, the Pioneer Klan of Roswell inaugurated its existence with a cross-burning in the city. In early January a large number of cars " . . . came down from South Hill at

1:30 o'clock in the morning. It is believed now that this was a meeting of the Klan," the *Roswell Daily Record* reported. All doubt was removed on 2 February 1924, when a "flaming red cross" was burned on South Hill; that is, just east of S. Main Street between Summit and McGaffey streets. A large number of cars were observed in the vicinity, which the *Alamogordo News* declared was the first known meeting of the Klan in Roswell. However, the *Roswell Daily Record* found that the cars were those of onlookers and not Klan members. It could be speculated that the cross-burning was in celebration of the imminent granting of the Roswell Klan's charter, which was approved in Atlanta three days later.[42]

As mentioned, on December 12, 1924, the District Attorney of Gainesville, Texas, Fred E. Wankan, and a KKK representative gave a lecture on "Americanism." Wankan was introduced by Frank Talmage. "Dr. E. T. Wilson, of the Seventh Day Adventists, first announced that the Adventists had given the use of the tabernacle to the Klan when asked for it, because they believed a lecture on 'Americanism' could not be bad. He disclaimed any affiliation with the Klan on the part of his membership." Wanken was grateful because the authorities of the Amory rejected him. The crowd packed the building "judging from the applause which was given the speaker, generally approved of his declaration."[43] Frederick Sager, pastor of the First Methodist Episcopal Church opened the meeting with a prayer. According to the account, the speaker disclaimed any hostility on the part of himself of the Klan against any race or religion, and asserted the purpose of the Klan was to foster Americanism, a love for the Flag, respect for and protection of American institutions, the Constitution, the protestant, gentile church the free public schools and generally to maintain white, Anglo Saxon supremacy in America.[44] Wankan maintained, the immigration of Mexicans were diluting the power of the "Asiatic races of Eastern and Southeastern Europe." KKK representative Wankan spoke for three and a half hours.[45]

Women were important to the Klan operation, for they had their own meeting and recruitment programs. For example, in the "Evening

Chats" section of the daily newspaper in Roswell there were numerous advertisements for women to attend lectures. In February 1925, Mrs. Louise Lynch, who was a national lecturer for the women of the Ku Klux Klan, held a meeting. The lecture was at the Capitan Theatre, "Monday night at seven thirty o'clock." Lynch was headquartered out of Little Rock, Arkansas, and established that she was not leaving until she had established the women's organization.

1925 A GREAT OIL PRODUCING

By May 1925, "Little Texas" had "Unlimited Possibilities As A Great Oil Producing Area."[46] Half of the Boyer family moved to Doña Ana County with Frank Boyer who happened to be delinquent in the taxes that he owed in Chaves County.[47] In June of 1925, fifteen thousand Klansmen paraded through the city of Washington, DC expressing its power, which paved the way for new recruits.[48] Roswell's KKK grew as more and more recruitment rallies were held in the name of "PATRIOTISM and LAW ENFORCEMENT."[49] Dr. H. F. Vermillion headlined the Public Lecture under the Auspices of the Knights of the Ku Klux Klan. It was a free lecture at the "Tabernacle" with no charge for admission. Rev. H. G. Vermillion was the former pastor of the First Baptist church of the city, but at the time was head of the Baptist sanitarium at El Paso.[50] According to the report,

> An unusual feature of this meeting was the appearance of approximately 100 Klansmen, in the full regalia of the order, marching into the tabernacle and taking their places behind the speaker on the platfrom [*sic*]. The men in hoods and robes, according to local Klan leaders were the members of the sixth division of the Roswell Pioneer Klan No. 15. Realm of New Mexico.[51]

Frank Talmage led the meeting, and "it was the first time that members of the Ku Klux Klan had been seen at a public meeting clad in the full dress of the order and as they marched into the building and onto the platform a complete silence fell on the huge gathering of both men and women who had gathered to hear the address."[52] King Kleagle C. L. Searmons, of the order for New Mexico and western Texas, was introduced by Dr. Talmage and outlined briefly the principles on which the order is founded and the purposes and aims of the organization. "Mr. Searmons removed his mask, but wore the robe of the order. At the conclusion of the meeting a cross which had been erected in front of the building was burned."[53] Dr. Talmage was the owner of the town mortuary that buried Roswellians including, in 1926, Henry Boyer, Frank Boyer's father.[54]

1926 BLACKDOM QUICK CLAIM DEED

As mentioned, in February 1926, Mrs. Louise Lynch, who was a national lecturer for the women of the Ku Klux Klan, held a meeting. The lecture was at the Capitan Theatre, "Monday night at seven thirty o'clock."[55] Lynch was headquartered out of Little Rock, Arkansas, and established that she was not leaving until she had established the women's organization. By 1926, the KKK was fully integrated into the fabric of Roswellian society. At the Grand Parade of Cotton Carnival, the Roswell KKK organized a float.[56] The weather was exceptionally pleasant, which brought out the largest crowd in the history of the parade.[57] Large Klan initiation classes were reported.[58] The Klan continued to recruit for years, advertising themselves as the "Patriotic Benevolent Organization" and "fraternal order of the Knights of the Ku Klux Klan."[59] Within the announcements:

> Membership in the Klan is obtained only through invitation. In the near future the SEVENTH DIVISION, comprising 175 men, it to be promulagated. Men interested and who can qualify to our requirements are solicited to send their names to address below and their requests will be considered and if agreeable, an invitation to them will be extended.

On February 24, 1926, Frank Boyer returned to Roswell to bury his father. The Blackdom Oil Company continued to produce speculation and royalty from land leases. There were announcements of deep tests in Blackdom.

In November 1926, the forty acres of Blackdom Townsite land transferred from Frank and Ella Boyer in a Quitclaim Deed to Crutcher Eubank. In a Quitclaim Deed, one transfers all the land without a warranty of the title and at no cost. The Blackdom townsite still functioned enough that it produced and needed new certified teachers like Cora Vandenbon in late 1926.[60] Also, more of Blackdom's land went under contract with the Gibson Oil Corporation, which drilled at Blackdom on the Hall No.1 well at a depth of seven hundred twenty feet in September.[61] In October, the Hall No.1 well was one thousand ninety-seven feet; they only hit salt water.[62]

> Centenarian Dies, Henry Boyer
> Henry Boyer, aged one hundred and three years, died at the home of his son, Henry Boyer Jr., on South Kansas Street, yesterday morning at ten o'clock. Henry Boyer was born in Hancock county, Georgia on October 29, 1822, on the plantation of Elias Boyer. His mother was Aggie Boyer, she being a slave who was born in Africa and brought to America by the early slaveholders. He was married to Hester Hill and from this union there are surviving four sons, John, Henry Jr., Robert S, and Frank. Also, one daughter Mrs. M. V. Johnson. He also leaves thirty-eight grandchildren. He was a member of the African Baptist Church, having joined them in 1876. Funeral services will be held tomorrow, afternoon at two thirty o'clock from the Colored Baptist Church with Rev. Wm. Profitt [*sic*] in charge of same and burial will be at South Park.[63]

1927 JUNETEENTH ANNIVERSARY

On May 9, 1927, Jackson M. Wagoner earned a patent for 320.75 acres, his first and the fourth homestead of the family. Together, the Wagoner family owned two square miles of Blackdom. The Afro-Frontier town continued to grow in land mass as the activity of the town decreased in the late 1920s.

The *Roswell Daily Record* reported a story headlined "Sixty-Two Years of Freedom Be Celebrated at Blackdom 19th":

> Our sixty-second Juneteenth anniversary is scheduled to arrive at Blackdom, Chaves County, New Mexico, on Sunday, June 19th, 1927.
>
> On that day, it is being arranged to have, instead of a jazz band to furnish music, a well-trained choir to sing the choicest of our "Plantation Melodies," as well as some of the latest negro spirituals. There will be preaching of course whether you like it or not. That means by the very nature of the thing that there will be no booze in three miles of town and certainly, none will be on the grounds if hoping will keep it away. In the plan, provision is being made to utilize every moment of time from start to finish in singing, praying, preaching, and lecturing on all important questions now agitating the minds of today.
>
> Room will be made on the program for school children from anywhere and everywhere, this giving our boys and girls an excellent opportunity to read or declaim in public.
>
> Everybody is hereby cordially invited to come and help swell the crowd. And don't forget if you come you are under ten thousand and one obligation to bring your eats with you if you think well of your appetites. Clinton Ragsdale will furnish barbecue, but this is a basket dinner.
>
> Come on Sunday, June 19th, 1927, dressed in your Sunday clothes and with your baskets running over with the best eats you ever prepared. So Long! Blackdom.

Blackdom was a thriving town as late as Juneteenth of 1927. The Blackdom population was divided; however, between the original Blackdomites and the newer more secular cohort. The new Blackdomites listened to jazz, but the elders of the town found the music devilish. Most divisive was the zero-tolerance alcohol policy in Blackdom during prohibition. A rural and urban divide began to solidify as the idea of Blackdom continued, but the reality as a town languished. Blackdomites owned vast amounts of land, but they came together in the town square less over time.

> Oil Test Near Blackdom
> Messrs. Warman and Meeler are moving a rig for a 2,000-foot test to the SW 1/4 sec 23 13-24, in the Blackdom area, west of Dexter and west of the Pecos river. It is understood plans have been made to drill an additional test, in event the first proves to be dry. It was learned here several weeks ago that a location had been made in this area.
>
> Mittie Held on Liquor Charges
> Mittie Moore Wilson, local negress, was arrested this morning by police officers on a charge of possession of intoxicating liquor. She interred a plea of not guilty when arraigned before Judge Winston and her trial was set for 10 O'Clock tomorrow morning. Officers said that they found a considerable quantity of liquor in her possession.[64]

The infamous reign of Mittie Moore Wilson continued into the mid-1930s.

ROSWELL DAILY RECORD
SEPTEMBER 13, 1929

Speculators needed credit and capital to survive when 1929 began with a mini-stock market crash. The major indices suffered tremendous loss in value, peaking in September. By August, major investors in oil speculation in Blackdom in need of capital began soliciting the public for investment.

1930 MITTIE, IN POLICE COURT

A complaint was filed this morning in Judge Winston's court by Mittie Moore Wilson against Eddie Moore, charging abuse and threats of violence. No disposition has been made in this case. Noma Sanders pleaded guilty to a charge of vagrancy and was given a fine of $17.50 which she paid. Edgar Below pleaded not guilty to a charge of reckless driving, the case being set for ten o'clock tomorrow.[65]

BLACKDOM OIL COMPANY C. 1930

Daily Observations by the Advertising Solicitor.
Sorry now that we read John Mullis's newspaper today. Everything was set for a nice easy day next Monday and here he goes and reminds our wives-that Labor Day would be the proper time for friend husband to do those odd jobs that have been accumulating for some time hope his wife makes him clean all the carpets and rugs in the house and paint the back porch.

The oil well at Blackdom is down 1,600 feet according to O. J. Wortman and it's going to take some jack to keep on drilling, for that reason Mr. Wortman is offering to take – any of us into partnership at two bucks an interest, you're at liberty to buy as many two dollar interest as you wish.

Stu. Hawley clipped 17hours from the record driving a Buick from Los Angeles and return, making the round trip in 144 hours and 44 minutes. Curl McNally says it took a Buick to do it and Grant Keys agrees with him, but insists that he couldn't have done it without using his Texaco oil. We haven't tried to break the record in person, so our opinion wouldn't be worth a whoop.

Remember the stores close at nine tonight and won't open again until Tuesday morning, except those shops that are open perpetually, so better stock up tonight. Monday, and the first of the month, what a joke on the bill collector, everybody will be away from town or hiding out serves 'em right anyway.

1932 CHAVES COUNTY ENTERS THE DEPRESSION

On February 27, 1932, the *Roswell Daily Record* reported:

> NOTICE OF SHERIFF'S SALE UNDER EXECUTION
> By virtue of an execution issued out of the District Court of Chaves County, New Mexico on the 25th day of January 1932, in the suit of (Flora Bell, Administratrix, plaintiff against Mittie Moore Wilson, defendant being No. 6799, on the Civil Docket of said Court, upon a judgment rendered in said cause in, behalf of plaintiff in the sum of $367.09, an interest and all cost. I have levied on the following described real estate as the property of said defendant to wit . . .
>
> Section 17 and 18, Township 14 South, Range 24 East, N. M. P. M., subject to mortgage of $462.50, in favor of Bloom Land and Cattle Company; also, lots 23, 25, 27, 29, and 31, Block 5, Thurbers Addition to City of Roswell, New Mexico, subject to a mortgage of $2988.30 in favor of Chaves County Building and Loan Association.
>
> Notice is hereby given that on the 24th day of March 1932, at the hour of 10 o'clock a.m. of said day at the West Front Door of the Chaves County Court House, I will sell said property, subject to said mortgages, to the highest and best bidder for cash to satisfy said execution.
>
> Dated this the 26th day of February, 1932.
>
> JOHN C. PECK, Sheriff.
> By E. L. Peck, Deputy.
> —Advertisement.

Woman Driver Hurt In Crash (1936)
Flagstaff, Aug. 30.--(AP)--Mittie Wilson, middle aged of Roswell, N.M., suffered serious injuries when her car and a wrecked machine being towed, sideswiped four miles east of Winona today.

The wrecked car belonged to Carl Tudor of Van Buren. Okla., and had been in a collision last night.

The Wilson machine struck a rear fender of the Tudor car and swerved from the road and overturned.

The woman was alone and was traveling east. She suffered cuts, abrasions and a possibly fractured skull.

Tudor and his father, Les Tudor are in a hospital here. Their condition is not believed serious.

A third car ran into the two cars that collided and overturned but continued toward California after being righted.[66]

Santa Fe New Mexican August 31, 1936
FLAGSTAFF -- Mittie Wilson, 201 South Virginia Ave Roswell suffered serious injuries yesterday east of Winona when her automobile and a wrecked machine being towed, were sideswiped.[67]

CHAPTER 7

THE CRASH & POSTSCRIPT

I wanted the history of the Blackdom Oil Company to die with me. I was angry. Writing has been a sacrifice and if not for the patience and partnership of Marissa Roybal this book would not have ever materialized. As a result of my many limitations, I needed help. To lift the veil of "history," some people are fully funded with an institution behind them and others find themselves fully educated and financially poor. Marissa believed when no one else cared that Blackdom's history was missing a decade. Marissa encouraged me to continue without "them." She understood the power of Afro-frontierism nurtured in this Blackdom narrative.

Experienced managing the performative, Marissa understood my instinct to bridge the gap between academic and the public grand narrative. Prior to partnering with Marissa, I began a public social media-based campaign. Our partnership fostered the opportunity to introduce my work in Santa Fe, New Mexico to reintroduce Black people in the Borderlands. Marissa understood there was potential for crossover into entertainment, and we continued to produce "edutainment"—a legacy of my childhood listening to M.C. KRS-1. Her historiographic significance begins with helping to institutionalize the Blackdom Thesis in the public square with the re-founding of the Blackdom Townsite Company in September 2019.

Marissa descends from fourteen-plus generations of Native New Mexicans who were homesteaders and farmers. Marissa's parents were raised and surrounded by family and community members in Santa Fe, Pojoaque, and Nambe who knew how to plant, grow, raise, make, build, or fix almost anything. In 1965, when Marissa joined the family, her maternal side continued to raise goats and chickens and cultivate fruit trees, vegetables, and flower gardens. There were still glimpses of her familial homestead life that once sustained them fully.

Marissa's parents moved to an ethnic, cultural, and socioeconomically diverse community in 1965: Butterfield Park, New Mexico. The proximity to the border and the White Sands Missile Range was a stark contrast to Santa Fe. Life in the unincorporated village of Butterfield was close to the border, dry, dusty, and illuminated her formative years.

The Blackdom Thesis helped Marissa answer questions about her family. Marissa saw the Afro-Frontier community as a microcosm of a larger system that unlocked a new history of New Mexico. Amid the continued and heightened violence against Black bodies in recent years, Marissa understood this history was relevant. She heard my effort to challenge the "tricultural" narrative and decided to work for Blackdom.

Intentionally, we incorporated The Blackdom Townsite Company to reintroduce Blackdom to New Mexico. Most recently, she worked as a program coordinator/community outreach at a non-profit, whose intent was largescale culture change: the activation of a culture of learning through which new forms of education, leadership, and organizational practice emerge and thrive; this allowed her to reflect, develop new skills, and bring the culmination of all her experiences forward into her work at The Blackdom Townsite Company.

Marissa, imbued with the value of self-sufficiency and an entrepreneurial spirit, puts her skills to work for the Blackdom Thesis as a tool for cultural change. As the Chief Operating Officer of Blackdom Productions LLC. and Blackdom Clothing Ltd. Co., she helps to deliver authenticated Blackdom narratives in whatever form people are willing to receive this new Black history.

Due to the tremendous amount of rejection, I stopped believing Blackdom had any significance. I had a vision, but if it had not been for Marissa's activation, Blackdom's boom times, a whole decade of history would have continued to be lost. Marissa's extensive representation, business, relationship building, and organizational skills as well as her personal history and passion made this book possible.

Significant to the Blackdom Thesis, Marissa associated the work we produced, the need for institution, and the ontological parallel with Blackdom Townsite Company of one hundred years ago. Analogous to the original Blackdomites, we built institutions to aid in the full recognition of the Blackdom Oil Company in the public narrative of Blackdom. Although I wrote a dissertation on the history of Blackdom and included my findings; nothing, I found a whole decade of new Black history and there was nowhere to appeal for the inclusion.

After a dramatic editing of my dissertation, I attempted to reshape Wikipedia's page on Blackdom, New Mexico. I quickly received a rebuke from the online platform's rejection department. I tried editing Wikipedia and was rebuffed by the site managers. For a short period of time, Quintard Taylor helped me disrupt Wikipedia's hold on Blackdom's public narrative. In the digital frontier, Dr. Taylor published my first 500-word essay on BlackPast.org, an institution and platform he founded.

Unbothered, I proceeded filling out job applications after my graduation. I then began to engage Facebook in my "spare" time. With no job prospects after graduation, I had a lot of "extra" time. Unknown to me and most people, Facebook automatically generates pages for locations when Wikipedia publishes them on their platform. My arrogance propelled me to engage this digital hegemonic power. I then felt the record needed to change out of respect for the people I spent a whole decade of my life trying to understand. My first act of rebellion against Wikipedia and Facebook was to dominate all posts connected to the platform's location check-in: Blackdom, New Mexico.

Considering few people on the planet had ever heard of Blackdom, and I had a lot of time at my disposal with no job prospects, most posts reflected a dissertation being composted. Few had ever heard of Blackdom or seen the current nothingness of what's there today. With a few posts using the location Blackdom, New Mexico, I owned the digital frontier space. My posts consisted of material about Blackdom and the Blackdom Thesis. I was then able to engage descendants with the new history.

In a world going digital, I decided to teach my daughter about Blackdom, and the digital universe allowed us a safe space to contextualize the real struggle of her father not having a job that paid a living wage. Kahtia, my daughter, turned 10 in 2017 and a narrow story of our lives began to emerge, digitally in Blackdom. Social media Blackdom was a proxy location that contextualized her lesson on how to thrive; as a child of a Black man (behind the Du Boisian Veil of double-consciousness). In a mixed media pedagogical approach and an experimental approach to curriculum, "we, I" began to imagine ourselves only existing in Blackdom. Looking through a child's eyes; distinct borders were blurry at best. From Las Cruces, New Mexico, where we lived, to El Paso where I went to school, she often slept for the whole 45-minute ride, to and fro. Never once did she recognize her world as it was; three states, two countries, and people failing to be one whole community.

Blackdom allowed us to virtually contextualize our reality. As a father who loved track and field, I began filming our time as coach and athlete on the track. In Facebook's virtual frontiers, our intentionality agitated Kahtia's consistent progress in real life. Recognizable on

Instagram was a documented case of how the idea of Blackdom had the potential to change a physical reality.

Composting my dissertation while contextualizing father/daughter time revealed my intentions in writing this book. Kahtia and I did not know the significance of our posting of her practices in Blackdom. Our collective actions, under the guise of Blackdom, agitated the intentional outcome of thriving an unbearable existence. The dual reality of living in the Borderlands shaped our intersection and proportionally mimicked our seamless transition into father/coach and daughter/athlete. The digital frontier provided a composite visual influenced by Blackdom Thesis.

After colonizing Facebook's digital frontier with videos, pictures and posts, Wikipedia had only accepted one of my pictures. Quintard Taylor reached out and asked that I consider an entry on Blackdom Oil Company. In 2020, although victory over Wikipedia eludes my digital Black colonization efforts, I answered Dr. Taylor's call to action in 2020 to immortalize Blackdomite society with a Blackdom Oil essay in celebration of its centennial. Due to copyright conversations in 2021, neither of my essays are currently on his platform. Prepared for the event of an unpublishing of my work, a contract for my first book was underway with Texas Tech University Press.

MAISON: THE MILITARY, MINISTRY, AND MASONRY

Maison Nelson loved me enough to show up to my doctoral graduation. In 2015, Maison took military leave to watch me walk across the graduation stage with a PhD and a mock diploma. Not until 2019 did Maison realize that the history I cultivated over decades of research, writing and writing, was real Black history. Maison had only consumed popular stories about Black history and could not reconcile what he "knew" with the history I produced. He thought I made "it" up in part because never did he hear me talk about what White people did. Centralizing the agency of Black folks in my Blackdom narrative the history appeared foreign in part because his expectation was that there was no lasting success in Black history one hundred years ago.

My role as the historian in the family was to redefine and reshape Black history for the lost generations who tuned out "the White man's history." Maison had little problem tuning out the community ethos about joining "the White man's military." His selective hearing had more to do with the profit motive for entering military ranks. Motivated by how much money he could make, the stability of military careers, and a desire to be a good patriarch he listened and heard what he needed to overcome community indoctrination.

My goal with this Blackdom history was in part an attempt to provide what needed to be heard to address American indoctrination that has marginalized information unconducive to the agenda of the "White" hegemonic power.

This is a humble attempt to address misconceptions about Black history, starting with the African diaspora and explaining how time and space operates on a continuum for Black folk. For Maison, I used what he understood about the Black Church and his belief in God (immutable) and the history of Ministers and their role in Black communities. Maison was a member of the military and he was exposed to the long history of Black folks using the military-industrial complex to transform the next generation. Most difficult for Maison was the Masonic element of Black history in general and Blackdom's history specifically.

Maison intersected with Freemasonry, but he had little context to process his intersection. He was approached by Freemasons to become a "traveler" and seek enlightenment. According to Maison, "it was weird." Maison went on to describe his discomfort with the thought of fraternity because "it seemed like a gang." I pressed my brother to find out more because I wanted to join the Prince Hall Lodge Frank Boyer and other Blackdomites established in the Borderland, I was rejected. Maison went as far as to emphasize that his name was pronounced "May Sawn" in part because that was how his mother Olivia said it. Also, his encounter alerted him of the serendipity of Maison sounding like mason, which was mentioned in his first contact with the organization. Freemasonry, as Maison understood, "wouldn't put no money" in his pocket so he decided not to engage.

Maison's community indoctrination was correct; Freemasonry would not directly put money in his pocket. As a father, Maison eliminated all material that had the potential to "mess up his money." Two years younger than me, 43 in 2021, he retired from the Air Forces with full benefits. He has a new job as a contractor for the military at the same base he worked. Arguably, Blackdom experienced a similar cultural shift during the 1920s when new Blackdomite leaders shifted to a more extractive understanding of themselves in relationship with the Afro-Frontier town.

This book is for the people who instinctively ignore history. In some ways Maison was proof of the Blackdom thesis and the power of an idea. Being there for someone is most important. We grew up in the age of crack. We kind of knew to expect a little crazy from family and for years my brother may or may not have believed I was crazy. Processing a decade's worth of doctoral work took time. In all fairness to Maison, I may have appeared mentally challenged. In fact, most people around at the time would find it easier to tell you about the few times I was lucid. My mind was in Blackdom, but my body was in the present day working through divorce, bankruptcy, and I ended up homeless in varying degrees.

From my humble beginnings on 48th and Western in Los Angeles to Santa Fe, New Mexico, in 2020, I have had a separate space to exist outside my circumstances. With my PhD and $200,000 in student loan debt, I now call it Blackdom. While Blackdom was a real place, I attempted to resurrect the idea of Blackdom, which detached me from reality even further. For the short time I was homeless and the long period I couldn't sustain a place to live on my own, Blackdom kept me moving when I just wanted to crawl under a rock and die. After I graduated with my doctorate, I sounded like a homeless man talking about this magical place called Blackdom. It was a weird time in my life, because I was a homeless man, talking about Blackdom. But Blackdom was a real place, and this book is a new Black history.

NOTES

INTRODUCTION

1. "Blackdom Made Location," *Roswell Daily Record*, September 1, 1920.
2. Walter Thompson-Hernández, "Evoking History, Black Cowboys Take to the Streets," *New York Times*, June 9, 2020; updated June 11, 2020.
3. Reginald Horsman, *Race and Manifest Destiny: The Origins of American Racial Anglo Saxonism* https://www.worldcat.org/title/race-and-manifest-destiny-the-origins-of-american-racial-anglo-saxonism/oclc/1041148870%26referer=brief_results (Cambridge: Harvard University Press, 2009).
4. "Vado Negro Leader Claims to be Head of Largest Family in State," *Las Cruces Sun-News*, March 30, 1947.
5. Kenneth Marvin Hamilton, *Black Towns and Profit: Promotion and Development in the Trans- Appalachian West, 1877–1915* (Urbana: University of Illinois Press, 1991).
6. Timothy E. Nelson, *The Significance of the Afro-Frontier in American History: Blackdom, Barratry, and Bawdyhouses in the Borderlands 1900–1930* (PhD diss., University of Texas at El Paso, 2015).
7. Hamilton, *Black Towns and Profit.*
8. Karl Jacoby, *The Strange Career of William Ellis: The Texas*

Slave Who Became a Mexican Millionaire (New York: W. W. Norton, 2017).

CHAPTER 1

1. "Vado Negro Leader Claims to be Head of Largest Family in State," *Las Cruces Sun-News*, March 30, 1947.
2. *Santa Fe New Mexican*, September 9, 1903.
3. Francis M. Boyer, *Homestead Entry Final Proof—Testimony of Witness: person name* (Land Office at Roswell, NM: February 23, 1905) Document No. 1173.
4. Nina Mjagkij, *Organizing Black America: An Encyclopedia of African American Associations* (New York: Garland, 2001), 204.
5. David Robertson, *Denmark Vesey: The Buried Story of America's Largest Slave Rebellion and the Man Who Led It* (New York: Knopf, 2000).
6. Nell Irvin Painter, *Exodusters: Black Migration to Kansas after Reconstruction* (New York: Knopf, 1977).
7. Edward Wilmot Blyden and Hollis Ralph Lynch, *Selected Letters of Edward Wilmot Blyden* (Millwood, N.Y.: KTO Press, 1978), 33.
8. Marcus Garvey and Amy Jacques Garvey, *The Philosophy and Opinions of Marcus Garvey, or, Africa for the Africans* (Dover, MA: Majority Press, 1986).
9. US Congress, Senate, Report and Testimony of the United States Senate to Investigate the Causes of the Removal of the Negroes from the Southern States to the Northern States, 3 vols., 46th Congress, 2nd Session, Senate Report 693, 1880.
10. Carter G. Woodson, *A Century of Negro Migration* (Washington, DC: Association for the Study of Negro Life and History, 1918).
11. *Evening Star* (Washington, DC), July 28, 1866. https://www.loc.gov/item/sn83045462/186607-28/ed-1/.
12. United States Supreme Court, *Ancient Egyptian Arabic Order of*

Nobles of the Mystic Shrine et al. v. Michaux et al., 1929.

13. *The Daily News*, [Huntingdon, Pennsylvania] April 10, 1928.
14. *St. Louis Post-Dispatch*, Sunday, March 26, 1922.
15. Wilson Jeremiah Moses, *Afrotopia: The Roots of African American Popular History* (Cambridge: Cambridge University Press, 2002).
16. Ariane Liazos and Marshall Ganz, "Duty to the Race: African American Fraternal Orders and the Legal Defense of the Right to Organize," *Social Science History* 28, no. 3 (2004): 485–534, http://www.jstor.org/stable/40267853, accessed July 18, 2021.
17. *Taylor County News* (Abilene, TX), May 3, 1895.
18. "American Negro Colony in Brazil," *Middletown Daily Argus*, June 12, 1895.
19. "A Negro Colony for Wyoming," *Denver Republican*, June 22, 1897.
20. "Negro Colony in Alabama," *Atlanta Constitution*, November 7, 1897.

CHAPTER 2

1. "New Mexico to Have Nigger Town," *Hereford Reporter* (Texas), October 16, 1903.
2. Elliott M. Rudwick, "The Niagara Movement," *The Journal of Negro History* 42, no. 3 (1957): 177–200, doi:10.2307/2715936, accessed July 18, 2021.
3. Christensen, S. (2007, December 16). *Niagara Movement (1905-1909).* BlackPast.org. https://www.blackpast.org/african-american-history/niagara-movement-1905-1909/
4. U.S. Senate. Special Committee of United States Senate on the Irrigation and Reclamation of Arid Lands, *Expenditure Authorizations and Requirements for Senate Committees* (Washington: Government Printing Office, 1890), 119.
5. Ira G. Clark, *Water in New Mexico: A History of Its*

Management and Use (Albuquerque: University of New Mexico Press, 1987), 68.

6. *Cornell Alumni News*, vol. 8 (September 1, 1905–August 31, 1906): 158.
7. In 1905, along with Frank Chisum of Roswell, Charles Childress of Roswell, John Montgomery of Dexter, George Hinson of Roswell, were witnesses on Isaac Jones's Final Homestead Proof.
8. Joseph Campbell, *The Hero with a Thousand Faces* (London: Sphere Books, 1975).
9. Maisha Baton and Henry J. Walt, *A History of Blackdom, N.M. in the Context of the African American Post Civil War Colonization Movement* (Santa Fe, NM: Historic Preservation Division, Office of Cultural Affairs, 1997).
10. Ibid.
11. Charlie Smith and Cindy Gaillard, *Blackdom*, Albuquerque, NM, KNME-TV, 1997.
12. "Vado Negro Leader Claims to be Head of Largest Family in State," *Las Cruces Sun-News*, March 30, 1947.
13. Letter to Leary, Gill, and Marrow from Frank Boyer, winter 1904, Historical Society for Southeast New Mexico.
14. Blackdom Townsite Company, *Articles of Incorporation*, 1903. art. 3, sec. 6.
15. "Articles of Incorporation," *Santa Fe New Mexican*, September 9, 1903.

CHAPTER 3

1. "William Proffit Dies," *Roswell Daily Record*, July 15, 1929.
2. *Roswell Daily Record*, December 12, 1924.
3. "Vado Negro Leader Claims to be Head of Largest Family in State," *Las Cruces Sun-News*, March 30, 1947.
4. Joshua 1:1–3 records the transition of Israelites into God's Promised Land.

5. Charlie Smith and Cindy Gaillard, *Blackdom*, Albuquerque, NM, KNME-TV, 1997.
6. *Santa Fe New Mexican*, October 1, 1903.
7. Isaac Jones, *Homestead Entry Final Proof -Testimony of Claimant*, Land Office at Roswell, February 23, 1905, Document No. 867.
8. US Bureau of the Census, Roswell, Twelfth Census of the United States: Schedule No. 1.–Population, New Mexico Territory, Chaves County, Sheet No. 21, 1900.
9. Charles Childress, *Homestead Entry Final Proof—Testimony of Witness: Isaac Jones*, Land Office at Roswell, NM: February 23, 1905, Document No. 867.
10. US Bureau of the Census, Roswell, Twelfth Census of the United States.

CHAPTER 4

1. W. E. B. Du Bois, *The Souls of Black Folk: Essays and Sketches* (Chicago: A. C. McClurg & Co., 1903).
2. W. E. B. Du Bois Papers (MS 312), Special Collections and University Archives, University of Massachusetts Amherst Libraries, Letter from Ruth Loomis Skeen to W. E. B. Du Bois, July 1920, describing the racial climate in New Mexico, requesting copies of *The Crisis* for a small town of African Americans called Blackdom.
3. *The Crisis*, 1929.
4. Moses, *Afrotopia*.
5. Wilson Jeremiah Moses, *The Golden Age of Black Nationalism, 1820–1925* (New York: Oxford University Press, 1988).
6. "50 Years Ago," *Albuquerque Journal*, February 14, 1965.
7. Martha Menchaca, "Chicano Indianism: A Historical Account of Racial Repression in the United States," *American Ethnologist* 20, no. 3 (1993): 583–603, http://www.jstor.org/stable/646643, accessed May 31, 2021.

8. Pablo Mitchell, *Coyote Nation: Sexuality, Race, and Conquest in Modernizing New Mexico, 1880–1920 (Worlds of Desire)* (Chicago: University of Chicago Press, 2005).
9. Alexandra Stern, *Eugenic Nation: Faults and Frontiers of Better Breeding in Modern America* (Berkeley: University of California Press, 2016).
10. "Organization of Blackdom," *Kokomo Daily Tribune* (Indiana), September 10, 1903.
11. *Hereford Reporter* (Texas), September 10, 1903.
12. Timothy E. Nelson, "Blackdom in the Borderlands: Significance of the Afro-Frontier (1903–1929)," *El Palacio* (Spring 2021).
13. *Houston Chronicle*, January 23, 2009.
14. W. C. Holden, "Experimental Agriculture on the Spur Ranch, 1885–1904," *Southwestern Social Science Quarterly* 13, no. 1 (1932): 16–23, http://www.jstor.org/stable/42864765, accessed June 4, 2021.
15. New Mexico Humanities Council, "Starting Conversations: Blackdom, NM," February 23, 2021.
16. Nelson, "Blackdom in the Borderlands."
17. Mark Mathabane, *Kaffir Boy: An Autobiography* (New York: Touchstone, 1998).
18. Nelson, "Blackdom in the Borderlands."
19. Holden, "Experimental Agriculture on the Spur Ranch, 1885–1904."
20. "Negro Thanksgiving," *Pecos Valley News* (Artesia, NM), December 7, 1911
21. Clinton Ragsdale, Homestead Entry Final Proof – Testimony of Claimant (May 27, 1913), no. 337606.
22. Mark Thompson, "Fact or Fiction? Did President Benjamin Harrison Really Try to Fire New Mexico Territorial Judge A.A. Freeman?", Bar Bulletin, January 15, 2007, Volume 46, No. 3.
23. *Las Vegas* (NM) *Daily Optic*, May 28, 1907.
24. Ibid.

25. *Los Angeles Herald*, June 24, 1905.
26. Ibid.
27. *Santa Fe New Mexican*, May 4, 1906.
28. *Santa Fe New Mexican*, May 7, 1906.
29. *Santa Fe New Mexican*, July 21, 1905.
30. California Superior Courts, *The Pacific Reporter* (St. Paul, MN: West Publishing Co., 1907), 731.
31. Regge N. Wiseman, Maisha Baton, and Yvonne Roye Oakes, *Glimpses of Late Frontier Life in New Mexico's Southern Pecos Valley: Archaeology and History at Blackdom and Seven Rivers* (Santa Fe: Museum of New Mexico, Office of Archaeological Studies, 2000), 9.

CHAPTER 5

1. Gary Webb, *Dark Alliance* (New York: Seven Stories Press, 2011).
2. James Brown, "It's a Man's Man's Man's World," Talent Masters Studios, New York, February 16, 1966.
3. Ice Cube (O'Shea Jackson Sr.), "A Bitch iz a Bitch," Los Angeles, California, Universal Music Group, Ruthless Records & Priority Records, November 6, 1987.
4. Carole Pateman, *The Sexual Contract* (Stanford, CA: Stanford University Press, 2018).
5. Emma Maggie Solberg, *Virgin Whore* (Ithaca, NY: Cornell University Press, 2018).
6. *Roswell Daily Record*, February 2, 1996
7. Maisha Baton, "The Community of Blackdom, N.M," *A Site Survey, Oral History, and Historic Review Project* (No. 35-95-10009.09), 8.
8. "Vado Negro Leader Claims to be Head of Largest Family in State," *Las Cruces Sun-News*, March 30, 1947.
9. Charles L. Harris, *Harris' Public Land Guide: A Compilation of Public Land Laws and Departmentalions Thereunder* (Chicago:

Peterson Linotyping Co., 1912), 133.

10. In November 1907, the Secretary of the Interior authorized the Soldiers' Additional Homestead Entry by Assignee. In Harris, *Harris' Public Land Guide*, 133.
11. Frank Boyer, assignee of Mattie Moore, alleged sole heir of Dickson Garner [dec'd], *Application Held for Rejection* (Washington, DC: Department of the Interior General Land Office, February 9, 1911).
12. Robert H. Nelson, *Public Lands and Private Rights: The Failure of Scientific Management* (Lanham, MD: Rowman & Littlefield, 1995), 29.
13. Thomas E. Sheridan, *Arizona: A History* (Tucson: University of Arizona Press, 1995), 141.
14. Frank Boyer, assignee of Mattie Moore, alleged sole heir of Dickson Garner [dec'd], *Application Held for Rejection* (Washington, DC: Department of the Interior General Land Office, February 9, 1911).
15. *Artesia Pecos Valley News*, December 7, 1911
16. *Santa Fe New Mexican*, December 30, 1911.
17. United States Register of the Department of Justice and the Judicial Officers of the United States (Washington, DC: US Government Publishing Office, 1871).
18. See Martha H. Patterson, *The American New Woman Revisited: A Reader, 1894–1930* (New Brunswick, NJ: Rutgers University Press, 2008), 177.
19. See Kidada E. Williams, *They Left Great Marks on Me: African American Testimonies of Racial Violence from Emancipation to World War I* (New York: New York University Press, 2012).
20. Anita Scott Coleman, *Unfinished Masterpiece: The Harlem Renaissance Fiction of Anita Scott Coleman* (Lubbock: Texas Tech University Press, 2008).
21. "Guilt Not Proven," *Roswell Daily Record*, November 1, 1917.
22. United States, The Abridgment . . . Containing Messages

of the President of the United States to the Two Houses of Congress . . . with Reports of Departments and Selections from Accompanying Papers (Washington, DC: US Government Printing Office, 1913), 804.

23. *City of Roswell v. Carman [Kyle]*, Violating Section 64 Ordinance 33, Being an Inmate of a Bawdy House, Volume 3 Police Judge's Docket No. 15 (June 25, 1914), 369, courtesy of Historical Society for Southeast New Mexico, Inc.
24. *City of Roswell v. Mittie Moore*, Violating Section 62 Ordinance 33, Keeping a Bawdy House, Volume 3 Police Judge's Docket No. 11 (June 25, 1914), 365, courtesy of Historical Society for Southeast New Mexico, Inc.
25. *Roswell v. Richardson*, 915-NMSC-079, 21 N.M. 104, 152 P. 1137 (S. Ct. 1915).
26. *Roswell v. Richardson*, 915-NMSC-079, 21 N.M. 104, 152 P. 1137 (S. Ct. 1915).
27. Susan G. Butruille, *Women's Voices from the Western Frontier* (Boise, ID: Tamarack Books, 1995), 137; Barbara Meil Hobson, *Uneasy Virtue: The Politics of Prostitution and the American Reform Tradition* (New York: Basic Books, 1987), 25.
28. J. Clay Smith, *Emancipation: The Making of the Black Lawyer, 1844–1944* (Philadelphia: University of Pennsylvania Press, 1993), 503.
29. *Rio Grande Republican* (Las Cruces, NM), August 11, 1916.
30. Toby Smith, *Little Gray Men: Roswell and the Rise of a Popular Culture* (Albuquerque: University of New Mexico Press, 2000), 21.
31. Eustace Boyer, Homestead Entry Final Proof–Testimony of Claimant (June 16, 1920), No. 035042.
32. *Roswell Daily Record*, August 29, 1919.
33. Scholars such as Alexandra Stern make the argument that during the World War I era medicalization and militarization were a tandem, particularly in the Borderlands. Alexandra

Stern, *Eugenic Nation: Faults and Frontiers of Better Breeding in Modern America* (Berkeley: University of California Press, 2005), 58.

34. *Roswell Daily Record*, February 7, 1917.
35. *Roswell Daily Record*, March 3, 1917.
36. *Roswell Daily Record*, March 3, 1917.
37. *City of Roswell v. Mamie Roberts*, Prostitution Ordinance 33 Section 64, Volume 5 Police Judge's Docket No. 347 (March 2, 1917), 237, courtesy of Historical Society for Southeast New Mexico, Inc.
38. *Roswell Daily Record*, March 3, 1917.
39. *Roswell Daily Record*, April 5, 1917.
40. Ibid.
41. City of Roswell Police Judge's Docket (March 31, 1917), 261, 264, and 267.
42. *City of Roswell v. Mittie M. Wilson*, Prostitution Ordinance 33 Section 64, Volume 5 Police Judge's Docket No. 381 (April 2, 1917), 271, courtesy of Historical Society for Southeast New Mexico, Inc.
43. United States, *Home Reading Course for Citizen-Soldiers* (Washington, DC: Government Printing Office, 1917).
44. *Roswell Daily Record*, August 29, 1917.
45. Ibid.
46. The 1915 critically acclaimed and President Woodrow Wilson–approved film, adapted from a novel titled *The Clansman*, was a propaganda tool for the war effort.
47. *Roswell Daily Record*, October 5, 1917.
48. *Roswell Daily Record*, August 4, 1917.
49. *Roswell Daily Record*, November 1, 1917.
50. *Roswell Daily Record*, December 5, 1917.
51. "Mittie Moore Here Again," *Roswell Daily Record*, December 5, 1917.
52. Ibid.

53. *Roswell Daily Record*, January 4, 1918.
54. "Negro Shoots—Misses," *Roswell Daily Record*, April 27, 1917.
55. Ibid.
56. Thomas Collins, Homestead Entry Final Proof–Testimony of Claimant (October 11, 1913), No. 022637.
57. Crutcher Eubank, *General Land Office Certificate of the Registry* (Roswell, NM, August 16, 1907), Patent No. 271166.
58. *Roswell Daily Record*, January 4, 1918.
59. *Roswell Daily Record*, January 5, 1918.
60. *Roswell Daily Record*, November 18, 1919.
61. "Negro Woman Doing Her Share of War Work," *Roswell Daily Record*, January 11, 1918.
62. *Roswell Daily Record*, April 8, 1917.
63. *Roswell Daily Record*, August 28, 1919.
64. "Will Pool Acreage," *Roswell Daily Record*, August 8, 1919.

CHAPTER 6

1. "Vado Negro Leader Claims to Be Head of Largest Family in State," *Las Cruces Sun-News*, March 30, 1947.
2. *Roswell Daily Record*, August 8, 1919.
3. Ibid.
4. Roswell was the major city and the county seat, with 7,033 residents of the total county population.
5. *Roswell Daily Record*, December 31, 1919.
6. *Roswell Daily Record*, December 10, 1929.
7. Ibid.
8. Ibid.
9. *Roswell Daily Record*, October 18, 1919.
10. Ibid.
11. Ibid.
12. *Roswell Daily Record*, December 31, 1919.
13. *El Paso Herald*, March 4, 1920.
14. *Roswell Daily Record*, April 7, 1920.

15. *Roswell Daily Record*, September 1, 1920.
16. *Roswell Daily Record*, November 29, 1920.
17. Ruth Loomis Skeen, "The Other Pocket," *The Crisis*, Crisis. United States: Crisis Publishing Company, November 1920; 126.
18. *Roswell Daily Record*, August 8, 1919.
19. *Roswell Daily Record*, January 2, 1919.
20. *Roswell Daily Record*, December 31, 1919.
21. *Roswell Daily Record*, January 11, 1919.
22. *Roswell Daily Record*, March 7, 1919.
23. *Roswell Daily Record*, August 8, 1919.
24. *Roswell Daily Record*, May 8, 1919.
25. *Roswell Daily Record*, January 31, 1919; *Roswell Daily Record*, February 5, 1919; *Roswell Daily Record*, March 12, 1919.
26. *Roswell Daily Record*, February 7, 1919.
27. Ibid.
28. *Roswell Daily Record*, August 28, 1919.
29. *Roswell Daily Record*, August 30, 1929.
30. *Roswell Daily Record*, February 16, 1920.
31. Ibid.
32. *Roswell Daily Record*, April 7, 1920.
33. *Fort Worth Star-Telegram*, April 11, 1920.
34. Donald R. Lavash, *A Journey Through New Mexico History* (Santa Fe, NM: Sunstone Press, 1993), 192.
35. *Roswell Daily Record*, August 28, 1919.
36. *Roswell Daily Record*, August 8, 1919.
37. Lavash, *A Journey Through New Mexico History*, 192.
38. *Roswell Daily Record*, September 13, 1923.
39. *Farmington Times Hustler*, September 7, 1923.
40. *Roswell Daily Record*, December 12, 1924.
41. Ibid.
42. Ibid.
43. Ibid.

44. Ibid.
45. Ibid.
46. *Roswell Daily Record*, May 6, 1925.
47. *Roswell Daily Record*, July 11, 1925.
48. *Roswell Daily Record*, June 17, 1925.
49. *Roswell Daily Record*, December 14, 1925.
50. *Roswell Daily Record*, December 16, 1925.
51. Ibid.
52. Ibid.
53. Ibid.
54. *Roswell Daily Record*, July 20, 1929.
55. *Roswell Daily Record*, February 6, 1926.
56. *Roswell Daily Record*, October 9, 1926.
57. *Roswell Daily Record*, October 14, 1926.
58. *Roswell Daily Record*, November 3, 1926.
59. *Roswell Daily Record*, December 1–4, 1928.
60. *Roswell Daily Record*, September 2, 1926.
61. *Roswell Daily Record*, September 20, 1926.
62. *Roswell Daily Record*, October 26, 1926.
63. *Roswell Daily Record*, February 24, 1926.
64. *Roswell Daily Record*, August 30, 1929.
65. *Roswell Daily Record*, January 6, 1930.
66. *Arizona Independent Republic*, August 31, 1936.
67. *Santa Fe New Mexican*, August 31, 1936.

BIBLIOGRAPHY

Adeleke, Tunde. *UnAfrican Americans: Nineteenth-Century Black Nationalists and the Civilizing Mission*. Lexington: University Press of Kentucky, 1998.

Aguirre Beltrán, Gonzalo. *Cuijla, Esbozo Etnográfico de un Pueblo Negro*. Mexico: Fondo de Cultura Económica, 1959.

Alexander, Charles. *Battles and Victories of Allen Allensworth*. Ann Arbor, MI: University Microfilms International, 1979.

Andújar Persinal, Carlos. *La Presencia Negra en Santo Domingo: Un Enfoque Etnohistórico*. Santo Domingo: [s.n.], 1997.

Appiah, Anthony, and Henry Louis Gates. *Africana: The Encyclopedia of the African and African American Experience*. New York: Basic Civitas Books, 1999.

Athearn, Robert G. *In Search of Canaan: Black Migration to Kansas, 1879–80*. Lawrence: Regents Press of Kansas, 1978.

Barnes, Kenneth C. *Journey of Hope: The Back-to-Africa Movement in Arkansas in the Late 1800s*. Chapel Hill: University of North Carolina Press, 2004.

Baton, Maisha, and Henry J. Walt. *A History of Blackdom, N.M. in the Context of the African American Post–Civil War Colonization Movement*. Santa Fe, NM: Historic Preservation Division, Office of Cultural Affairs, 1997.

Beito, David T., and Linda Royster Beito. *Black Maverick: T.R.M.*

Howard's Fight for Civil Rights and Economic Power. Urbana: University of Illinois Press, 2009.

Bennett, Herman L. *Africans in Colonial Mexico: Absolutism, Christianity and Afro-Creole Consciousness, 1570–1640*. Bloomington: Indiana University Press, 2005.

———. *Colonial Blackness: A History of Afro-Mexico*. Bloomington: Indiana University Press, 2009.

———. *Lovers, Family and Friends: The Formation of Afro-Mexico, 1580–1810*. PhD thesis, Duke University, 1993.

Berry, Mary Frances. *My Face Is Black Is True: Callie House and the Struggle for Ex-Slave Reparations*. New York: Alfred A. Knopf, 2005.

Beyan, Amos Jones. *African American Settlements in West Africa: John Brown Russwurm and the American Civilizing Efforts*. New York: Palgrave Macmillan, 2005.

———. *The American Colonization Society and the Creation of the Liberian State: A Historical Perspective, 1822–1900*. Lanham, MD: University Press of America, 1991.

Bittle, William E., and Gilbert Geis. *The Longest Way Home: Chief Alfred C. Sam's Back-to-Africa Movement*. Detroit: Wayne State University Press, 1964.

Blyden, Edward Wilmot, and Samuel Lewis. *Christianity, Islam and the Negro Race*, by Edward W. Blyden, with an Introduction by Samuel Lewis. London: W. B. Whittingham, 1887.

Bontemps, Arna. *Great Slave Narratives*. Boston: Beacon Press, 1969.

Branch, William B. *Crosswinds: An Anthology of Black Dramatists in the Diaspora*. Bloomington: Indiana University Press, 1993.

Burin, Eric. *Slavery and the Peculiar Solution: A History of the American Colonization Society*. Gainesville: University Press of Florida, 2005.

Byfield, Judith A., LaRay Denzer, and Anthea Morrison. *Gendering the African Diaspora: Women, Culture, and Historical Change in the Caribbean and Nigerian Hinterland*. Bloomington: Indiana

University Press, 2010.

Carroll, Patrick James. *Blacks in Colonial Veracruz: Race, Ethnicity, and Regional Development*. Austin: University of Texas Press, 2001.

Castillo, Susan P. *American Literature in Context to 1865*. Chichester, West Sussex, UK: Wiley-Blackwell, 2011.

Cha-Jua, Sundiata Keita. *America's First Black Town: Brooklyn, Illinois, 1830–1915*. Urbana: University of Illinois Press, 2000.

Chaves County (NM). *Chaves County Comprehensive Land Use, Planning and Zoning Report*, 1973.

Clegg, Claude Andrew. *The Price of Liberty: African Americans and the Making of Liberia*. Chapel Hill: University of North Carolina Press, 2004.

Conniff, Michael L., and Thomas J. Davis. *Africans in the Americas: A History of the Black Diaspora*. New York: St. Martin's Press, 1994.

Crockett, Norman L. *The Black Towns*. Lawrence: Regents Press of Kansas, 1979.

Curry, Dawne Y., Eric D. Duke, and Marshanda A. Smith. *Extending the Diaspora: New Histories of Black People*. Urbana: University of Illinois Press, 2009.

Deagan, Kathleen A., and Darcie A. MacMahon. *Fort Mose: Colonial America's Black Fortress of Freedom*. Gainesville: University Press of Florida, 1995.

Dodson, Howard, and Colin A. Palmer. *Ideology, Identity, and Assumptions*. New York: New York Public Library, 2007.

———. *Origins*. New York: New York Public Library, 2008.

Gaspar, David Barry, and Darlene Clark Hine. *Beyond Bondage: Free Women of Color in the Americas*. Urbana: University of Illinois Press, 2004.

Gomez, Michael Angelo. *Diasporic Africa: A Reader*. New York: New York University Press, 2006.

———. *Exchanging Our Country Marks: The Transformation of*

African Identities in the Colonial and Antebellum South. Chapel Hill: University of North Carolina Press, 1998.

———. *Reversing Sail: A History of the African Diaspora*. Cambridge: Cambridge University Press, 2005.

Gradwohl, David M., and Nancy M. Osborn. *Exploring Buried Buxton: Archaeology of an Abandoned Iowa Coal Mining Town with a Large Black Population*. Ames: Iowa State University Press, 1984.

Guidry, Frank. *Forging Diaspora: Afro-Cubans and African Americans in a World of Empire and Jim Crow*. Chapel Hill: University of North Carolina Press, 2010. http://public.eblib.com/EBLPublic/PublicView.do?ptiID=837907.

Hall, Gwendolyn Midlo. *Africans in Colonial Louisiana: The Development of Afro-Creole Culture in the Eighteenth Century*. Baton Rouge: Louisiana State University Press, 1992 [revised edition 1995].

Hamilton, Kenneth Marvin. *Black Town Promotion and Development on the Middle Border, 1877–1914*. PhD thesis, Washington University, 1979.

———. *Black Towns and Profit: Promotion and Development in the Trans-Appalachian West, 1877–1915*. Urbana: University of Illinois Press, 1991.

Hamilton, Ruth Simms. *Creating a Paradigm and Research Agenda for Comparative Studies of the Worldwide Dispersion of African Peoples: Proceedings of the International Advisory Committee of the African Diaspora Research Project, November 9–11, 1988*, 1990. Copies available from the African Diaspora Research Project, Urban Affairs Programs, Michigan State University.

———. *Routes of Passage*. East Lansing: Michigan State University Press, 2003.

———. *Routes of Passage: Rethinking the African Diaspora*. East Lansing: Michigan State University Press, 2007.

Hanger, Kimberly S. *Bounded Lives, Bounded Places: Free Black*

Society in Colonial New Orleans, 1769–1803. Durham: Duke University Press, 1997.

Harris, Joseph E. *Abolition and Repatriation in Kenya*. Kampala: East African Literature Bureau, 1977.

———. *African-American Reactions to War in Ethiopia, 1936–1941*. Baton Rouge: Louisiana State University Press, 1994.

———. *The African Diaspora*. Chicago, IL: Rand McNally & Co., 1992.

———. *The African Diaspora Map*. Worcester, MA: Clark University Cartographic Service, 1990.

———. "African Diaspora Studies: Some International Dimensions." *Issue: A Journal of Opinion* 24 (1996): 6–8.

———. *The African Presence in Asia: Consequences of the East African slave trade*. Evanston, IL: Northwestern University Press, 1971.

———. *Africans and Their History*. New York: Meridian, 1998.

———. *Afro-American History Interpretation at Selected National Parks*. Washington: Howard University, Dept. of History, 1978.

———. *Arbitration versus Strikes*. Pittsburgh, PA: Watkins & Co, 1941.

———. *The Coast African Association: African Politics on Kenya's coast, 1940–1955*. Nairobi: East African Literature Bureau, 1976.

———. "A Comparative Approach to the Study of the African Diaspora." *Global Dimensions of the African Diaspora* (1982): 112–24.

———. *East African Slave Trade and Repatriation in Kenya: A Lecture at Howard University, April 8, 1974*. Washington: Howard University, Dept. of History, 1974.

———. *Global Dimensions of the African Diaspora*. Washington, DC: Howard University Press, 1993 [1982].

———. *The Kingdom of Fouta Diallon*. Thesis, Northwestern University, 1965.

———. *Perspectives on the Changing Relationship between Afro-Americans and Africans*. Khartoum, Sudan: Institute of

African and Asian Studies, University of Khartoum, 1976.

———. *Repatriates and Refugees in a Colonial Society: The Case of Kenya*. Washington, DC: Howard University Press, 1987.

Harris, Joseph E., and James Mbotela. *Recollections of James Juma Mbotela*. Nairobi: East African Pub. House, 1977.

Harris, Joseph E., Alusine Jalloh, and Stephen E. Maizlish. *The African Diaspora*. College Station: Texas A&M University Press for the University of Texas at Arlington, 1996.

Hermann, Janet Sharp. *The Pursuit of a Dream*. New York: Oxford University Press, 1981.

Hine, Darlene Clark, Trica Danielle Keaton, and Stephen Small. *Black Europe and the African Diaspora*. Urbana: University of Illinois Press, 2009.

Hine, Darlene Clark, and Jacqueline McLeod. 1999. *Crossing Boundaries: Comparative History of Black people in Diaspora*. Bloomington: Indiana University Press, 1999.

Hood, Aurelius P. *The Negro at Mound Bayou, Being an Authentic Story of the Founding, Growth and Development of the "Most Celebrated Town in the South," Covering a Period of Twenty-Two Years*. Nashville, TN: AME Sunday School Union, 1910.

Horne, Gerald. *Black and Brown: African Americans and the Mexican Revolution, 1910–1920*. New York: New York University Press, 2005.

Horne, Gerald, and Mary Young. *W. E. B. Du Bois: An Encyclopedia*. Westport, CT: Greenwood Press, 2001.

Hornsby, Alton. *Black America: A State-by-State Historical Encyclopedia*. Santa Barbara, CA: ABC-CLIO, 2011.

Hunwick, John O., and Eve Troutt Powell. *The African Diaspora in the Mediterranean Lands of Islam*. Princeton: Markus Wiener Publishers, 2002.

Jones, John Maxwell. *Slavery and Race in Nineteenth-Century Louisiana-French Literature*. Camden, NJ: Jones, 1978.

Johnson, Hannibal B. *Black Wall Street from Riot to*

Renaissance in Tulsa's Historic Greenwood District. Austin, TX: Eakin Press, 1998. http://search.ebscohost.com/login.aspx?direct=true&scope=site&db=nlebk&db=nlabk&AN=27658

King, Wilma. *Stolen Childhood, Second Edition Slave Youth in Nineteenth-Century America*. Bloomington: Indiana University Press, 2011. http://public.eblib.com/EBLPublic/PublicView.do?ptiID=713669.

Knight, Frederick C. *Working the Diaspora: The Impact of African Labor on the Anglo-American World, 1650–1850*. New York: New York University Press, 2010.

LeMay, John. *Chaves County*. Charleston, SC: Arcadia, 2009.

Lewis, Bernard. "The African Diaspora and the Civilization of Islam." In *African Diaspora: Interpretative Essays*, edited by Martin L. Kilson and Robert I. Rotberg, 37–56. Cambridge, MA: Harvard University Press, 1976.

Littlefield, Daniel F. *Africans and Seminoles: From Removal to Emancipation*. Westport, CT: Greenwood Press, 1977.

Litwack, Leon. *Black Leaders of the Nineteenth Century*. Urbana, IL: University of Illinois Press, 1991.

Manning, Patrick. *The African Diaspora: A History through Culture*. New York: Columbia University Press, 2009.

Michigan State University, and Ruth Simms Hamilton. *Creating a Paradigm and Research Agenda for Comparative Studies of the Worldwide Dispersion of African Peoples: Proceedings of the International Advisory Committee of the African Diaspora Research Project, November 9–11, 1988*. East Lansing, Mich. (W-142 Owen Graduate Center, Michigan State University, East Lansing 48824): The Project, 1990.

Moses, Wilson Jeremiah. *Afrotopia: The Roots of African American Popular History* Cambridge: Cambridge University Press, 2002.

———. *The Golden Age of Black Nationalism, 1820–1925*. New York: Oxford University Press, 1988.

National Negro Business League (US). *National Negro Business*

League: A New Program for Greater Service. Norfolk, VA: Guide Pub. Co., 1927.

Nelson, Vaunda Micheaux, and R. Gregory Christie. 2009. *Bad News for Outlaws: The Remarkable Life of Bass Reeves, Deputy U.S. Marshal*. Minneapolis: Carolrhoda Books.

New Mexico. *1990 Affirmative Action Information, Chaves County*. Albuquerque, NM: The Bureau.

New Mexico. 2003. *Chaves County Health Profile . . . New Mexico County Health Profiles*. Santa Fe, NM: The Office, 2003.

Obichere, Boniface I., and Jacob Drachler. *Black Homeland, Black Diaspora: Cross-Currents of the African Relationship*. New York: National University publications, 1975.

Ogundiran, Akinwumi, and Toyin Falola. *Archaeology of Atlantic Africa and the African Diaspora*. Bloomington: Indiana University Press, 2007.

Okpewho, Isidore, Carole Boyce Davies, and Ali Al'Amin Mazrui. *The African Diaspora: African Origins and New World Identities*. Bloomington: Indiana University Press, 1999.

Otey, Frank M. *Eatonville, Florida: A Brief History of One of America's First Freedmen's Towns*. Winter Park, FL: Four-G Publishers, 1989.

Painter, Nell Irvin. *Creating Black Americans: Africa-American History and Its Meanings: 1619 to the Present*. Oxford: Oxford University Press, 2007.

———. *Exodusters: Black Migration to Kansas after Reconstruction*. New York: Knopf, 1977.

Palmer, Colin A. *Human Cargoes: The British Slave Trade to Spanish America, 1700–1739*. Urbana: University of Illinois Press, 1981.

———. *Slaves of the White God: Blacks in Mexico, 1570–1650*. Cambridge: Harvard University Press, 1976.

Porter, Kenneth Wiggins, Alcione M. Amos, and Thomas P. Senter. *The Black Seminoles: History of a Freedom-Seeking People*. Gainesville: University Press of Florida, 1996.

Presbyterian Church in the U.S.A. *Home Mission Monthly*. New York: Woman's Board of Home Missions of the Presbyterian Church in the U.S.A., 1886.

Riley, Glenda. *Taking Land, Breaking Land: Women Colonizing the American West & Kenya, 1840–1940*. Albuquerque, NM: University of New Mexico Press, 2003.

Robinson, Pearl T., and Elliott P. Skinner. *Transformation and Resiliency in Africa: As Seen by Afro-American Scholars*. Washington, DC: Howard University Press, 1983.

Rodriguez, Junius P. *Encyclopedia of Slave Resistance and Rebellion*. Westport, CT: Greenwood Press, 2007.

Rosas Mayén, Norma. *Afro-Hispanic Linguistic Remnants in Mexico: The Case of the Costa Chica Tegion of Oaxaca*. PhD thesis, Purdue University, 2007.

Rosemont, Franklin, and Robin D. G. Kelley. *Black, Brown, & Beige: Surrealist Writings from Africa and the Diaspora*. Austin: University of Texas Press, 2009.

Schwartz, Stuart B. *Slaves, Peasants, and Rebels: Reconsidering Brazilian Slavery*. Urbana: University of Illinois Press, 1992.

Schwendemann, Glen. 1971. *Nicodemus: Negro Haven on the Solomon*. Topeka: State of Kansas Commission on Civil Rights, 1971.

Segal, Ronald. *The Black Diaspora*. New York: Farrar, Straus and Giroux, 1995.

———. *Islam's Black Slaves: The Other Black Diaspora*. New York: Farrar, Straus and Giroux, 2001.

Shepherd, Verene. *Working Slavery, Pricing Freedom: Perspectives from the Caribbean, Africa and the African Diaspora*. New York: Palgrave, 2002.

Szanton, David L. *The Politics of Knowledge: Area Studies and the Disciplines*. Berkeley: University of California Press, 2004.

Thwaite, Daniel. *The Seething African Pot: A Study of Black Nationalism, 1882–1935*. Westport, CT: Negro Universities

Press, 1970.

Turner, Glennette Tilley. *Fort Mose: And the Story of the Man Who Built the First Free Black Settlement in Colonial America*. New York: Abrams Books for Young Readers, 2010.

Tyler-McGraw, Marie. *An African Republic: Black and White Virginians in the Making of Liberia*. Chapel Hill: University of North Carolina Press, 2007.

United States. *Important Farmlands, Chaves County, New Mexico*. [Albuquerque, NM]: The Service, 1981.

Washington, Booker T. *The Negro in Business*. Boston: Hertel, Jenkins, 1900.

Wiseman, Regge N., Maisha Baton, and Yvonne Roye Oakes. *Glimpses of Late Frontier Life in New Mexico's Southern Pecos Valley: Archaeology and History at Blackdom and Seven Rivers*. Santa Fe, NM: Museum of New Mexico, Office of Archaeological Studies, 2000.

Uya, Okon Edet. *Black Brotherhood, Afro-Americans and Africa*. Lexington, MA: Heath, 1970.

———. *From Slavery to Public Service: Robert Smalls, 1839–1915*. New York: Oxford University Press, 1971.

———. *Historia de la Esclavitud Negra en las Américas y el Caribe*. [Buenos Aires, Argentina]: Claridad, 1989. http://books.google.com/books?id=MX64AAAAIAAJ.

Woodson, Carter Godwin. *The History of the Negro Church*. Washington, DC: Associated Publishers, 1921.

INDEX

ABOUT THE AUTHOR

Dr. Timothy E. Nelson was born in South Central Los Angeles, was raised in Compton, California during the early 1990s, and went to Santa Monica Community College in the wake of race and class-based conflict with the Los Angeles Police Department. Dr. Nelson played football at Compton High School, Compton Community College, and Santa Monica College before transferring to New Mexico State University, where he was awarded a scholarship. He graduated from New Mexico State University with a Bachelor's degree in U.S. History. Continuing to maintain ties with Compton, Dr. Nelson set up an admissions program to bring high schoolers from Compton to New Mexico State University.

During his time completing a master's degree in Black History at the University of Northern Iowa, Dr. Nelson also earned a commission as an officer in the US Army. He earned his PhD from the University of Texas at El Paso. He was the Racial Justice Director at the YWCA El Paso del Norte Region—the largest YWCA in the United States. He is also a proud charter member of his chapter of Phi Beta Sigma, whose motto is "Culture For Service and Service For Humanity."

Through his 2015 dissertation as well as his current outreach, Dr. Nelson's goal is uncovering and advocating for untold stories through various forms of art: academic books, trade books, screenplays, painting, photography, videography, and digitally applying his theory of colonization within the digital frontier.

Printed in the USA
CPSIA information can be obtained
at www.ICGtesting.com
CBHW020227210524
8864CB00002B/85